DEAR FRIEND,

I am pleased to send you this copy of *The Top 100 Questions*.

If you've ever wanted biblical answers to difficult questions about God, the universe, or what Christians believe, you'll find them here. This book gives short, clear answers to the most-often-asked questions, along with explanations of 50 difficult Bible passages. Author Richard Bewes, pastor of All Souls Church in London, is a longtime friend of my father, and his books are undiscovered spiritual treasures.

If you would like to know more about the Billy Graham Evangelistic Association, please contact us by calling toll-free, 1-877-247-2426. We would appreciate knowing how this book or our ministry has touched your life.

May God bless you.

Sincerely,

Franklin Graham
President and CEO

RICHARD BEWES

THE TOP 100 QUESTIONS

BIBLICAL ANSWERS TO POPULAR QUESTIONS
PLUS EXPLANATIONS OF
50 DIFFICULT BIBLE PASSAGES

This *Billy Graham Library Selection* special edition is
published by the Billy Graham Evangelistic Association with
permission from Christian Focus Publications.

CHRISTIAN FOCUS
Good Books with the Real Message of Hope

Scripture quotations marked (NIV) are from The Holy Bible, New International Version. Copyright ©1973, 1978, 1984, by International Bible Society. Used by permission of Hodder and Stoughton, a member of the Hodder Headline Group. All rights reserved. 'NIV' is a registered trademark of International Bible Society. UK trademark number 1448790.

Scripture quotations marked (ESV) are from The Holy Bible, English Standard Version, published by HarperCollins Publishers ©2001 by Crossway Bibles, a division of Good News Publishers. Used by permission. All rights reserved.

This book was written and first published in the United Kingdom, and the original spellings and phrases have been retained.

ISBN 1-59328-022-X
Previous ISBN 1-85792-680-3

© Copyright Richard Bewes 2002

Published in 2002
by
Christian Focus Publications, Ltd.
Geanies House, Fearn, Tain,
Ross-shire, IV20 1TW, Great Britain.

www.christianfocus.com

Cover design by Jarod Sutphin

Contents

Part Three: The Bible we read...................97

Part Four: The way we behave............139

Part Five: The Christ we follow............181

Introduction

Finding oneself on the receiving end of questions is a regular way of life for anyone who is applying the truth of the Bible to our modern, questioning world. Yes, it has to be the Bible! And the questions and answers that feature in these pages are drawn from a myriad of public meetings, a syndicated newspaper question column I used to run, late-night conversations, youth events, dinner parties, radio phone-ins, letters from enquirers, and innumerable encounters at the church door.

Here now is a new collection of questions and answers! In fact, I am submitting them as *the top hundred* that seem to be surfacing in our twenty-first century. I must emphatically declare that this book in no way attempts to present a coherent systematic body of teaching. These are simply answers to questions I have been given. Nevertheless, by dividing these pages into several sections, we can together cover a fair range of life, belief and experiences that provoke us into asking 'Why?', 'What?' and 'How?' I hope, too, that readers will value the closing appendix, on the top fifty *Difficult Bible Passage Questions* that have puzzled Christians over the years. Some of these only require a paragraph or two of explanation.

As far as Bible passages that I quote, I shall use a variety of available versions, including the King James Version (KJV) and the English Standard Version (ESV). **Please look up the references** where space forbids me to make the Bible quotation in full.

I am grateful to those who kindly endorse this book with their generous comments. I am also grateful to my secretary, Miranda Lewis, and our Resource and Communications Co-ordinator, Pam Glover, for their great help while this book has been in preparation. And I am *always* grateful to Anne Norrie and my ever-patient publishers at Christian Focus.

Richard Bewes
Written at All Souls Church,
Langham Place, London

Part One

The universe we inhabit

'*And God saw that it was good*'. In these words we see the approval of God stamped upon his work. For God did not merely discover that his work was good after he had finished it, but he teaches us that it is good....There cannot be a higher author, a more effectual instrument, or a more excellent reason, than God, his Word, and his creation of the good.'

The City of God,
Augustine of Hippo AD354–430

1. One universe or many?

Is Jesus Christ 'IT'....or is He only part of something yet bigger still? Are there other systems out there, alien to our own?

The answer to the question lies in the nature of Christ himself. He is the key to the whole of our existence. The Christian apostle Paul sums up the divine purpose vividly: *'...to bring all things in heaven and on earth together under one head, even Christ'* (Ephesians 1:10).

Why a universe, and not a series of 'multiverses'? Christ is the single, unifying reason. As two student leaders – Tom Parsons and Stephen Nichols – once explained in a Bible study at All Souls Church in London, 'Even the origin of the **university** (Latin: *'uni'* – one; *'veritas'* – truth) reflects the vision of a single coherent story, *one truth*. From the beginning, all subjects in our campuses – physics, music or mathematics – were separate chapters in one over-arching story, slices cut from one cake.'

But in recent years a widespread loss of confidence has resulted in a growing collection of highly diverse and irreconcilable 'stories'; there are as many narratives as there are narrators – 'my' story, 'your' story, the Marxist story, the feminist story. The university curriculum has widened to bizarre dimensions. 'You can even do courses in *Star Trek*', say Tom and Stephen, 'or studies on the career of some football star!' The idea that there could be *one* story that explains all the rest – a single factor, an individual Person – is dismissed as naïve.

But this is nothing new. The Christian apostles were up against the most fragmented world-view imaginable. There was Delphi with its oracle, the rites of the Egyptian god Isis, and Cybele, the mother of gods in Asia. Romans could go to Greece and identify their own Jupiter with Zeus, or visit Syria and find him in Baal. Yet this whole edifice was to crumble.

As the message of Christ took hold – by whose 'blood' all things on earth or in heaven could be made *one* (Colossians 1:20) – a new and unprecedented unity of thought began to take over. Tatian, the second century Christian leader, spoke of the relief of exchanging the tyranny of 10,000 gods for the benign monarchy of *one*. Augustine, two centuries later put it, 'This Child of the manger fills the world.'

The apostle Paul put it still more dramatically: 'He who descended is the very one who ascended higher than all the heavens, in order to fill the whole universe' (Ephesians 4:10). By this, Paul meant that there is no part of the universe that is free from Christ's control. Secondly, there is no room for anyone else. Diana, Mithras, Jupiter, Osiris and Venus had to go. Jesus has taken all the space! Thirdly, the ascension of Jesus implies, not a Christ-deserted world, but a Christ-*filled* world.

There is just one great universe – and Christ is its explanation and goal.

2. Are we on our own?

Gyorgy Mandics, a UFO expert from Timisoara in Romania, was reported to have learnt 17 foreign languages, in the hope that he could speak to any aliens who might land on earth. 'I'm sure', he said, 'that aliens exist, and I will be one of the few people able to communicate with them when they arrive' *(London Metro,* 15 June 2001).

But no such arrival will take place, because aliens do not exist. Gyorgy could have spared himself the trouble. And however fascinating the information that comes to us from the scientific exploration of the universe, our scientists could save themselves a great deal of nail-biting suspense and perhaps money, if they realised that the possibility of alien life is zilch. *We are alone in the universe.* But why can we be so sure on this issue?

The answer is found in a biblical world-view. At the centre of all existence is the one true God, who has focused his loving purposes upon the apex of His created universe – a race of beings, made in His image, and made for fellowship with Him. Planet Earth was to be the focal point of God's work. There, we possessed the capacity to worship, love, create and govern. To us was entrusted the care of the created order (Genesis 1:27,28). Thus when we as creation's chief actor, led by the original first pair, fell into rebellion, the entire cosmos was necessarily affected, and remains in a state of discordant tension and 'groaning' to this day (Romans 8:19–22).

Is there another 'system' outside of ours; another race of beings – which perhaps has never sinned and doesn't need salvation? No; the destiny of the solitary universe was integrated with the human race – a one-off group of beings created with God-like moral responsibility. As custodians, we stood alone. *When we fell, everything else shuddered.* And now all creation waits – along with us – for the final day of redemption through Christ (Romans 8:19).

It's Christ, the second Person of the eternal Trinity, who clinches the issue. Coming as God, to be born into our world as a human being, and to save the world through His death, He is at the right hand of God the Father. There He rules at the centre of everything, as representative of all humanity – not as a resurrected spirit but in a glorified body; not as an *ex-man* but as true and perfect Man, on behalf of His redeemed church.

Here is a consistent, unified picture. What of alien beings, then? They're not in the frame at all. In the Scriptures we learn of angels, but they are not aliens; they are an integral part of the created order, and have a part to play as God's messengers and servants.

It's official, then. Apart from the loving presence of God Himself, we are on our own in the universe.

3. Dwarfed by the distances?

Earth: '....a medium–sized planet, orbiting round an average star in the outer suburbs of an ordinary spiral galaxy, which is itself only one of about a million million galaxies in the observable universe. Yet the strong anthropic principle would claim that this whole vast construction exists simply for our sake. This is very hard to believe...'

(Stephen Hawking, *A Brief History of Time*, Bantam Press)

Hard to believe? It's impossible to believe....but for the authoritative witness of the biblical record that can stand outside and astride all our history and scientific probings – and endure the test of time.

For it is the Bible that gives us our proper perspective, and corrects the flaw in Stephen Hawking's world-view, notwithstanding his academic brilliance. Omitted from Hawking's statement are three factors, all of which are vital to the argument.

First, there is the factor of **God**-centredness, not **man**-centredness, in all our fantastic universe. Secondly, Hawking omitted to recognise that Creation is the home, not just of the human species as such, *but of a race of God-like beings*. That is our calling, and there is none higher. Thirdly, we must not forget that the whole of Creation centres in...a man, who, in the New Testament, is described in these terms:

He is the image of the invisible God, the heir over all creation. For by him all things were created: things in heaven and on earth, visible and invisible, whether thrones or powers or rulers or authorities; all things were created by him and for him. He is before all things, and in him all things hold together (Colossians 1:15–17).

Here we discover that the universe was created for Jesus Christ, fully God and fully man – representing as He does the prototype human being. It is only in relationship to Him, that our residence in the immensity of our cosmic surroundings begins to lose its absurdity.

Science has tended to point to the stages following the original 'big bang' – in the formation of continents, oceans, vegetation and the animal kingdom – as taking place over many millions of years. So vast are the figures, that our own significance and comparatively short history are reduced virtually to vanishing point.

But the Bible reverses that proportion and turns it round completely.

– 'The forming of the continents? The tortuous procedures, the millions of years that are said to lie behind those first jellies, crustaceans, and mosses? The dinosaurs and crocodiles? A week's work – that's all! We'll give that bit a page....well, perhaps two pages!'

– 'And the *real* story; God's plan and focus through a family, and His mission to the nations that those experts of yours dismiss as a perfunctory blip? Why, we'll need something like a thousand pages before we're through!'

It's this divine word that puts the balance straight and gives us orientation – *and size.*

FOR FURTHER STUDY of our human beginnings, see **Genesis** in the 'Book by Book' video studies, with guest contributor Anne Graham Lotz: enquiries: vestry@allsouls.org (for USA, www.visionvideo.com).

4. Who are we? What are we?

The question was raised by the statement of the Rev. Don Cupitt, a liberal clergyman and theologian who had ceased to believe in the objective reality of God: 'My self is a mere temporary aggregation of processes', he wrote. 'My own desires are part of the flux of forces in nature.' (From Scott Cowdell's *Atheist Priest?*, SCM Press)

Well....try telling that to the judge when you are up on a criminal charge; that, after all, you were no more than a collection of biochemical reactions – and that he too is another such collection – and see what happens! In a world where people are generally held responsible for their actions, the dogged attempts to interpret all wrong-doing as genetically derived – or as a kind of treatable disease – look pathetically shallow.

There is in every human being an element that says *I ought*. That relates to the image of God that was created in humanity from the beginning:

> So God created man in his own image, in the image of God he created him; male and female he created them (Genesis 1:27).

Genesis introduces us to the personal God of spirituality and relationship. It is impossible to understand ourselves as people, without this divine backcloth. True, like the animals we are creatures of common chemicals – we come from the 'dust' (Genesis 2:7). But 'the breath of life' was breathed into us in a way that seems to be different from the animation of the animal kingdom. Genesis 2:7 is the filling out and the counterpart of Genesis 1:27. In every person there is a spiritual capacity – for worship, prayer, and accountability. It is this truth that explains not only what we are, but *who* we are.

We are placed above the animals, and in charge of them, not by dint of brute force, but as managers of the earth's resources – naming and categorising the species (the beginning of zoology and science; Genesis 2: 19,20).

We are in the image of God – with a spiritual nature – but we are only images! *We are not God Himself;* we exist only by derivation and creation. In this we are unlike Jesus Christ who is the 'exact' replica of God (Colossians 1:15).

This is why New Age teaching eventually fails. It is of little use telling business executives in their seminars that they 'have a god within' and that there's nothing that they cannot do. Within six months they will discover that they have deadlines to chase, targets to achieve and duodenal ulcers – and that manifestly they are *not* God!

Nevertheless, every human being possesses something of the divine **image**. It is this that explains generosity, courage or selflessness, even among the irreligious. Anthropologists have used terms such as *homo sapiens* and *homo erectus* to describe humanity. It was my longstanding neighbour of many years, Dr John Stott, who coined the title *homo divinus*. That divine image has been there from the beginning – albeit severely defaced since humanity's rebellion (see chapters 6 and 7).

5. A woman's place?

Why was the first woman created second, as only a 'helper' for the man? This seems to place women on a lower footing altogether.

Let's be careful, first, not to be shackled, either by chronological rigidity or wooden literalism, as we look at the Genesis account of our beginnings. Actually, it's Genesis 1:27 that gives us the definitive, over-arching statement, where the man and the woman counter-balance each other, side by side:

> So God created man in his own image, in the image of
> God he created him; male and female he created them.

The account of chapter 1 is filled out and amplified by the details of chapter 2. If we are made in the image of God – who is a Trinity of Beings in **community** – so with us: *It is not good for the man to be alone. I will make a helper suitable for him'* (Genesis 2:18). It is not 'singleness' that is not good, but *solitude*.

1. The founding principle

There it is, in verse 18. Does 'helper' suggest a lower rank, with Adam as the Skipper of the ship and Eve as a sort of First Mate? Not if you check through a Bible concordance. The majority of Bible references where the same Hebrew word *(ezer)* occurs, are used to describe the kind of 'help' that only *God* can give (eg 1 Samuel 7:12; Psalm 121:2; Hosea 13:9).

So Eve, far from being an 'assistant', represents the vital God-given dimension that provides the human race with its astounding factor of what we can only call **'otherness'**. George Gilder has written, 'The differences between the sexes are the single most important fact of human society' (*Sexual Suicide,* Bantam, 1973, p.63).

2. The crowning mystery

After Adam has catagorised the animals, he is then introduced to 'the woman'. At this point he does not get out his notebook and exclaim, 'A new species! What shall we call it?' No, this is the electric moment of recognising his other half! The love poem that follows is surely the first in all history (Genesis 2:23).

So Eve is not taken out of 'the ground' – thus forming a new and separate kind of being. She is taken out of Adam's side, because men and women were to be of the very same essence. Exactly how the divine operation was performed we shall never know, because Adam was unconscious while it was happening!

3. The defining charter

Look now at Genesis 2:24: *For this reason a man will leave his father and mother and be united to his wife, and they will become one flesh.* This is the creational charter of **marriage** for all time – endorsed by Jesus (Matthew 19:5) – in which members of the two sexes can find intimacy and union, matched with (not against) each other as life partners (see chapter 73).

Human life should never consist in a battle of the sexes. Christian marriage is to be an illustration of *mutual submission,* one to the other (Ephesians 5:21).

6. Can you explain evil?

I get so discouraged by the evil on every side; the conflicts that seem to mount up, the undisciplined youth, corrupt leadership and terrorism worldwide. Where does it all come from? I see no hope.

In spite of everything that we see, there is hope! But *only* if we look for the answer in the Scriptures. Here are the briefest of guidelines:

1. Evil represents a defection, not a first cause

The original and eternal factor is represented by God alone – and his goodness. Evil is an intrusion into the universe, resulting from *an angelic rebellion* under a created angel, who aspired to be God himself (Isaiah 14:12–15; Ezekiel 28:11–19) – colluding simultaneously with *humanity's bid for independence*, as expressed by our spiritual ancestors, Adam and Eve (Genesis 3). These two acts of rebellion are part of one and the same fall.

Fellowship with the Creator was never something that could be programmed or enforced; if you are free to love, then you are also free to rebel. So evil entered, not as something that had always existed, but as a deviation, a rebellion from the original first cause. Augustine of old wrote:

> The evil angels, though created good, became evil by their voluntary defection from the good, so that the cause of evil is not the good, but defection from the good. (*The City of God*, Book 12)

2. Evil is headed by a counterfeit, not an absolute

Satan, who has a variety of names, is not an absolute being. He is neither all-powerful, all-knowing, or all-present. The opposite to Satan is not God, but *Michael*, leader of the angelic hosts (Revelation 12:7). Satan is a usurper and imitator. 'Satan's purpose', wrote Billy Graham, 'was not to make Eve as ungodly as possible, but to make her as godlike as possible – without God' (*Approaching Hoofbeats*, Word, p.105). As a created being, then, the Devil had a beginning, and he will have an end (Revelation 20:10).

3. Evil produces monotony, not creativity
Genesis 3:14–19 portrays the result of evil's entry in terms of dust, death, pain, thorns and thistles. Our whole environment – of which we are custodians – is affected (Romans 8:19,20). Because evil lacks the spark of original creativity, it can ultimately produce only a desert, a 'ground zero' wasteland. When education, medicine, politics and the arts ignore God, decline and confusion can be expected.

4. Evil ends in defeat, not triumph
The whisper of evil's downfall is already there in Genesis 3:15, with the divine announcement to the serpent of 'enmity' between the woman's future offspring and his own. The woman's 'offspring' is not plural, but singular – one Person! '**He** will crush your head' (the implication of defeat), 'and you will bruise his heel' (KJV). Even then, the serpent would only be *permitted* to bruise Christ, insofar as 'it pleased the Lord to bruise him' (Isaiah 53:10). The cross would ensure evil's defeat.

Be encouraged. History and the future belong to us!

7. Why am I stuck with Adam?

I don't see why we must all be branded as sinners as a result of a mythical action by two people. I wish to dissociate myself from Adam and Eve.

This was put to me during a phone-in programme. First, we must question the use of the word *mythical*. It's evident from the New Testament that Jesus believed in the existence of Adam and Eve (eg Matthew 19:4). Also, without the account of Genesis 3, we would be baffled as to what had happened between chapters 2 and 4; the transition from harmonious innocence to murderous hatred, and the growing crescendo of evil followed.

We cannot pretend that nothing had happened. Some have spoken of the Fall as though it was a step *upwards,* as Adam and Eve 'decided for themselves' towards 'maturity'. But no; here was a decision – not between good and evil (for they didn't know what evil was), but rather between themselves and God. In the wake of this decision comes death, disturbance and disintegration – and all of us are involved.

It was a real choice. If we complain that they should not have been created with the capacity to choose, we are really asking that they should have been created as plants or animals, because the fellowship with God that we were created for would not be fellowship at all, if it can be programmed into us.

Then we have to remind ourselves that Adam and Eve were not simply the first humans; they were *prototype* humans. You can make jelly for a children's party by pouring it into a mould, for it to cool. Every jelly that results will have the same shape. If, of course, you drop the mould and it becomes dented, all the jellies from then on will show up the flaw. *So with the first pair.* The image of God is still there, but it is flawed and dented, right through the entire race, universally.

And you wish to be dissociated from Adam and Eve? **That is good news.** According to the Bible, there are only two representative characters you can be identified with; one is Adam, the other is Jesus Christ – who is the 'second Adam' (Romans 5: 12–16):

> Just as the result of one trespass was condemnation for all, so also the result of one act of righteousness was justification that brings life for all (v.16).

Certainly we can't say that the sin in the Garden had nothing to do with us and it wasn't our fault, because we weren't there. We were there! But the other side is seen in the words of the old spiritual: *Were YOU there, when they crucified my Lord?* And the forgiven believer says, 'Yes! I was there. My sins – in which I have consistently concurred with the sin of Adam – were dealt with at the Cross....and from now on I am part of a second race. I am bound up now with *Christ'.*

8. Extra-terrestrial beings?

How seriously should we regard the theories that God was an astronaut, and that what Ezekiel saw in chapter 1 of his prophecy was a spacecraft?

As a start, please look at chapter 2. How fascinating – the possibility of what today might be called an Unidentified Flying Object? And that is just it – it *is* an area of fascination and speculation.

And commercialism too! This field of interest drew in many adherents with the publication in the last century of such books as von Daniken's *Chariot of the Gods?* and Hal Lindsay's *The Late Great Planet Earth*. These, and a proliferation of other speculative books, coupled with television programmes and Internet web sites exclusively devoted to the topic, have successfully turned the UFO dream into an *industry*.

Are we surprised? We should not be. For years Marshall MacLuhan, back in the 1950s and 1960s, was forecasting a reaction to the arid landscape presented by 'Modernity' – with its utilitarian, earthbound view that tended to close the sky off, and put humanity in a limiting, secularised straitjacket.

The next era, he said, would be 'religious'. And while scientism and the old one-dimensional modernity are well in evidence, 'Post-modernity' has lifted the lid off our world, with an array of differing 'narratives' and interpretations of life. It has affected architecture, fashion, the arts and, of course, people's view of what might be 'out there'. *There are no restrictions!*

The space-craft theory of Ezekiel reveals an interesting mindset. The throne on which the Son of Man is sitting (Ezekiel 1:26) is said to be the pilot's seat.

There is a yearning here – and it is understandable. First, materialism alone failed to satisfy; and here, apparently, is a world-view that lifts readers to dimensions and hopeful possibilities beyond their present horizons. Secondly, it is presented popularly, in a way that will attract school children, PhDs and lorry drivers alike. Thirdly, it is presented undemandingly. There is no cost or effort involved in following the gospel of space-fiction; your intellect is tickled and your hopes are vaguely raised. No moral choices are involved and no adjustment to your lifestyle is called for.

Christians should lean out with warmth – but with truth – towards the advocates for extra-terrestrial beings. *'You're onto something!'* should be our reaction. *'There IS another dimension above and beyond what we can see around us. And what you're onto just might be a first stepping stone to the Ultimate Reality!'*

And then we should begin to point to God, the only true God, who is behind the visions and super-normal appearances featured in the Bible. But he is a God who presents us with the supreme adventure of becoming members of a City that is going to last for ever. And it is a City which will descend upon us, from above, historically, right here upon Planet Earth. Turn them to Revelation 21:2....and they'll see. We must *all* get ready!

9. The creation of viruses?

If God created all things, why did he create these terrible viruses?

All forms of life would originally have been perfect. Let's understand that straight away; also that even today some bacteria are positively beneficial. Indeed, what many people drink every day – to aid their digestion – is no more nor less than a form of bacteria. We would not be able to digest our food properly without certain bacteria in our gut.

This understanding needs to be in the background of any discussion around your question. It is since the fall of humanity that disease, decay and death have intruded upon our existence. We have only to read, in Genesis chapter 5, the repeated occurrences of the phrase *And then he died* – to take in the inevitability of death, and its causes. The viruses of which you speak would have been a part of this universal phenomenon. What can we learn from them?

1. They instil a sense of humility
Long before the electron microscope had identified the virus, the very presence of disease and infection was a constant reminder that we are subject to death. None of us escapes; a hundred years or so – and there's a clean sweep right across the planet. Certainly the answer has been found to some of these viruses, but there is no denying that, however long we live, it is usually some infection that finally kills us. But consider this too:

2. They instil a sense of eternity
Not in themselves, of course. But repeatedly a virus attack will cause us to look up and around for answers. This heightens the possibility of our becoming exposed to the one factor that can give us real pointers – the revelation

that God has given us, culminating supremely in Jesus Christ. Many millions of people never even began to think about God and his saving plan, until they or a loved one were struck by an apparently random disease.

Focus on the virus alone – and the mystery may seem insoluble; but if we can stand a little further back, we can learn to view the fallenness of our situation through the wide-angle lens of God's revelation. Without that revelation we could never have known of his loving purposes.

3. They instil a sense of humanity

If God declared war on evil, pain and death – and he has clearly done so in Christ – then we must allow the presence of such infection and disease to provoke us into fighting them in his name. When I was a boy growing up in Africa, poliomyelitis was a feared scourge among us. How thankful we should be that there were researchers dedicated to ridding the world of this and other viruses. Christians can, and should, stand in firm support of them, with love as our motivation, and the resurrection as our confidence.

10. Where do animals fit?

What is the purpose of animals in our world? How do they tie in with the human race?

Despite the love of many for animals, the tendency of thinking people has been, on the whole, to minimise their importance in the divine scheme. This may partly be due to the influence wielded by Aristotle, the Greek philosopher and scientist (384–322 BC). He regarded animals as virtually on the same level as plants – and his thinking has left its stamp upon the western world.

But it may be said even of the animals that, like humanity, they too were endowed with 'the breath of life' (Genesis 6:17), although not bearing the divine image. Considerable emphasis is given in Genesis chapters 6–9 to the divine regard for the animals which were created in magnificent profusion and stupendous variety. Their relationship to the Creator is highlighted in the psalmist's celebration of creation (Psalm 104). This is a planet which is teeming with wild life of every kind – whose protection and conservation is part of the divine mandate to the human race.

We should take careful note that, after the Flood, God establishes his covenant with Noah and his descendants and with 'the birds, the livestock and all the wild animals...every living creature on earth' (Genesis 9:8–11).

To a high degree we would not be able to get along in life without the aid of animals. They help to run the world! The flowers are pollinated by the bees, the soil is aerated by the worms, the ground is fertilised by the herds, and even in the day of the internal combustion engine there are vehicles or ploughs pulled by animals that are stronger than ourselves. In all of the human responsibility to till the earth and look after it, the vast majority of the work has been done by animals. We may be the managers, but we would be lost without these, our partners.

If we wonder why some of the angelic beings in the Bible have the appearance of animals (eg, the living creatures of Ezekiel 1:4–14 and Revelation 4:6–8), one answer may be that what the animals are to us – as helpers – so the angels are to God.

So will there be animals in the new heaven and the new earth? *Can I expect to see my pet in the next life?* To ask such questions is to be setting too small an agenda, to be bringing God's wonderful future down to the level of our present familiar life. In effect we are saying, 'I want to carry on just as before.'

The next life will be so overwhelmingly wonderful (1 Corinthians 2:9), that such issues will fade from view. Certainly we would expect our future existence to be superior to the present in every way – the animals might indeed be included (Isaiah 11:6–9). But these are no more than hints, for the Bible is a book addressed primarily to the *human* situation.

11. Who or what are angels?

My 'New Age' friends talk a lot about angels. What are they?

There is plenty to learn. The Bible has far more to tell us about angels than New Age ever could!

1. Angels are worshippers around God's throne

They belong to a heavenly order of spiritual, though created beings, separate from God and therefore not to be worshipped. Essentially, they attend upon God in worship and praise. At the limited times when they have become visible (as in special divine visitations, or in prophetic visions) they reflect the awesome holiness and harmony of heaven (Daniel 7:9,10; Revelation 5:11,12).

2. Angels are executors of God's will

They are numerous and may be known by different terms (*holy ones, messengers, sons of God*). The 'cherubim' (plural of 'cherub') are presented in Scripture as winged creatures, flying to fulfil God's commands, guarding the way to his presence and acting as conveyors of his throned Person (Psalm 89:5; Genesis 3:24; Exodus 25:18–22; Ezekiel 1:4–24).

3. Angels are witnesses to God's saving acts

They are in evidence around the time of Jesus' birth, death, resurrection and ascension. They will be his heralds at his final return. They are said by Jesus to rejoice at the repentance of a sinner, and he speaks of them as finally gathering in his redeemed people (Luke 2:8–15; 22:43; 24:4–8; Acts 1:10,11; 1 Thessalonians 4:16; Luke 15:10; Matthew 24:30,31).

4. Angels are messengers at times of revelation

Angels have acted as announcers at the beginning of God's great eras – at the commissioning of prophets, at the start of the Gospel story, and at the inclusion of Gentiles in the church. These announcements were variously received, with awe, fear, astonishment and joy (Isaiah 6:1–7; Luke 1:26–33; Acts 10:1–8).

5. Angels are protagonists at times of conflict

The Bible teaches of an angelic rebellion and fall under Satan, 'the serpent', 'the Devil', 'the father of lies' and 'Accuser'. Although his defeat was assured by the victory of Christ's death, evil itself will not be finally banished until his destruction (Luke 10:18; 2 Kings 6:17; Daniel 12:1; Revelation 12:7–9).

6. Angels are ministers at times of crisis

At many points of God's dealings with his people, both patriarchs, prophets, apostles and indeed Jesus himself received ministry and help from angels at particular moments of stress, temptation or danger.

All believers may receive their protection and support. While we may be grateful for their presence, they are not to be reverenced as intermediaries between us and God. An undue attention to angels can lead to distortions of the faith (Genesis 19:15; 1 Kings 19:5–7; Matthew 4:11; Acts 12:7–10; Hebrews 1:14; Colossians 2:18).

Postscript: Old Testament accounts of 'the' Angel of the Lord (see chapter 29) refer to the Second Person of the Trinity, Christ – the 'Sent One' – in his pre-incarnate existence (eg, Genesis 16:7; 22:11; Exodus 3:2).

FURTHER STUDY: '*Open Home, Open Bible*' video series, cassette 6, programme 1 (enquiries@allsouls.org; for USA www.visionvideo.com)

12. How big was the flood?

A Mesopotamian disaster, or a world catastrophe? The Flood continues to fuel speculation worldwide.

That is the precise point – we don't even have to explain which flood we're talking about; Noah's Flood is firmly embedded in the human memory on every continent.

There is a *Hindu tradition* about a great flood, and a ship of safety finally landing on a northern mountain. *In China*, Fa-he, the reputed founder of Chinese civilisation, is represented as escaping from the waters of a deluge – and reappears as the first man in a new world, accompanied by his wife, three sons and three daughters; eight people in all. There is the famous *Babylonian Epic of Gilgamesh* with its detailed myth-legend of a great flood. *The Fiji islanders* have accounts of a flood, in which a family of eight was saved. In *South America*, paintings have been discovered, representing a flood, a man and his wife on a raft, with a mountain featuring in the story, as well as a dove. The *Cherokee Indians* have a similar story. Only Africa seems to be without a traditional flood story.

Our contention is that the book of Genesis gives us the original, inspired and definitive account of this mega event. It could have been Shem, one of Noah's sons, who later told his children of this great epic of his life, and as the human race fanned outwards from Mesopotamia, so the story travelled outwards as well – inevitably becoming garbled in the process, and mixed up with legend and folklore.

How big was the Flood, then? The right answer is that it was of all-time, universal dimension and significance. Certainly we can make out a strong case for a literal world-wide flood – with the release of the great waters both from below and above (Genesis 7:11,12). But we may also observe that the phrase of Genesis 7:19 – that 'all the high mountains under the entire heavens were covered' can be paralleled by Acts 2:5, where – on the Day of Pentecost – those who were present were *'from every nation under heaven'*. Those nations are then listed out in detail, and they are all from the then known world of Luke the writer – around the Mediterranean basin. So the Flood itself *need* not have extended across the entire world.

Can we respect the differing views among reverent students of Scripture? If we cannot, we are in deep trouble. Once we get into lengthy and heated debates as to whether the flood covered every dot of land-space on the world, we are in serious danger of exhausting ourselves and diverting people from hearing the *real* message of the Flood. What is it?

First, it widens the problem – from a garden to the whole world! The Flood conveys a universal warning. Second, it produces a model – for our entire understanding of judgment and grace, for ultimately the safety of the ark is found in Christ. Third, it sets the stage – for the drama of salvation that is to be unfolded from Genesis 12 onwards.

13. In touch – through Yoga?

How far does Yoga provide a valid way to meditate and be at peace with the world and the universe?

The word *Yoga* means 'union', and in Hindu philosophy the person who practises it does so to gain in self-control, but more importantly to reach union with the Infinite – who/which can be perceived variously.

Thus, even though the recruit to a Yoga class may be reassured that the exercises are 'non-religious', it still represents a Hindu world-view. 'Yoga', says one of its top advocates, 'is not a Friday night or Sunday morning practice; it is an entire way of life, and should occupy 24 hours of every day'. The little 'popular' books on Yoga never tell you that! In Yoga we are presented with:

1. An alternative interpretation of the universe

'Position One', in a standard book, begins with: 'Mantra: Om adi deva nameh. Here we face the spiritual son. Standing upright with the breath suspended, fully composed, we represent Purusha, the primeval god Adi Deva, at the very beginning of time'.

The basic Yoga 'Lotus position', in which a circle is made of thumb and forefinger – implies the unbrokenness of life in a never-ending circle of successive reincarnations. But that is not how the Christian sees life on this world (Hebrews 9:27). Just to read Colossians chapter 2 gives us the answer. Then how does Yoga view the divine?

2. A degraded image of God

Another quote: 'This posture, Hanum-an-asana....*Hanuman* was the name of a powerful monkey chief who was the son of Anjana and the devoted friend and servant of Rama, the seventh incarnation of Vishnu....'

A contrast with Colossians 2:6–10 shows the main difference between the basically Hindu concept behind Yoga, and the revealed truth of God in Jesus Christ. To go down the Yoga route is to make a shift towards a pantheistic standpoint, in which God is identified with nature, and finally towards a monistic view, in which God is conceived as an impersonal 'It', without form or personality.

3. A negative view of personhood

Again I quote: 'You will literally be moving, being in the nothing. The experience of nothing is Yoga'.

But the art of emptying one's mind is foreign to the Christian – who focuses the individual not upon Nothing, nor even upon ourselves, but upon Christ (Colossians 3:1,2). Paradoxically, in finding Christ we discover ourselves, and our identity becomes enhanced with the fullness of life that he promises (Colossians 2:10).

4. A deviant way of Redemption

The 'sin' question is never raised in Yoga, and the answer to sin – the Cross of Christ – is never in view. Rather, it is 'enlightenment' for the ignorant that is offered.

Breathing exercises and meditation (upon Christ and his Word) are commendable. But we are unwise to open the door for the entry of a system that in Paul's words, causes someone to lose connection with the Head, Christ Himself (Colossians 2:19).

14. Back into the past?

What is the Christian to make of claims to the remembrance of a previous life, or of events that took place even centuries earlier – that are then independently corroborated?

The subject of retrocognition is a very fascinating one, and a good deal has been written about it.

One of the most famous instances involved two women (both of high intelligence) who claimed, when walking in the Garden of Versailles in France, to have stepped back from 1901 to 1789. They 'saw' paths, buildings and even fashions that precisely corresponded to those of an earlier age. Naturally stories like this are open to challenge. Perhaps the Christian makes several thoughtful observations.

1. We are children of our own time
That is, our lives are set within a time process. They are given us as a one-off, never-to-be-repeated challenge. 'Only one life is allotted us', wrote Alexander Solzhenitsyn, 'one small, short life!' And we are told to make the most of the present opportunity (Ephesians 5:16).

Other eras have their fascination for us, and we can learn from them, but just now *we* are on the stage, and the potential of the present must not be weakened by time-consuming speculation. However:

2. We are children of eternity
God 'has put eternity into man's mind' (Ecclesiastes 3:11). And God, in whose image we are made, does indeed know the end from the beginning. So it is not too surprising if sometimes individuals have received a reminder – if no more than a whisper in a dream – of the divine and eternal context of their creation; inklings of transcendence, flashes of insight

into things that have happened (or may yet happen) outside of our present time span. The secular humanist will never understand this, but we do, knowing that we are 'fearfully and wonderfully made' (Psalm 139:14).

3. We are children of accountability
The second half of Ecclesiastes 3:11 tells us that God has limited us so that we cannot find out what he has done from the beginning to the end. We are not know-alls. And any insight into our eternal dimension carries with it a moral responsibility.

Deuteronomy 29:29 expresses it perfectly: 'The secret things belong to the Lord our God, but the things revealed belong to us and to our children for ever, *that we may follow all the words of this law.*' God himself would reveal certain of his secrets to the prophets of old. They used their perception, to point people to the Lord. This is quite different from the activity of the clairvoyant or fortune teller, which has no support in Scripture.

If there is a *biblical* retrocognition, it will be in operation at the final Judgment, when 'the books are opened', and men and women will be able to look back upon their past life – *this life.* There is no reincarnation, no other life that should occupy our attention, because it is appointed to us **once** to die, and after that, the judgment (Hebrews 9:27).

15. Did the sun stop still?

Can you help me over Joshua 10:12–14, about the sun standing still during Joshua's battle? I guess God *could* stop the world moving round if he wanted to. But did he?

Let's rely supremely on the Bible itself, rather than fly immediately to the scientists or archaeologists! The answer will be right here. As regards relating passages, significantly there is no reference to an astronomical act of God, either in Isaiah 28:21 – where the victory at Gibeon is quoted – or in the exploits of faith in Hebrews 11. There is a possible *allusion* only in Habakkuk 3:11.

Sure, the elements were on Joshua's side! It is reminiscent of Judges 5:20: *The stars in their courses fought against Sisera.* Here the quote is from the 'lost' book of Jasher, celebrating Israel's heroes: *O sun, stand still over Gibeon, O moon, over the Valley of Aijalon.*

Question: Was Joshua wishing for more daylight, in order to make certain of victory? If so, classical students will see a similarity in Agamemnon, who prays that the sun may not go down till he has sacked Troy. **Or, was Joshua, in fact, wishing for a little more *darkness*?** The comment of verse 13 doesn't at first glance read like that. 'The sun stopped in the middle of the sky and delayed going down about a full day.'

But as I look at the earlier report of the battle, I am made to think again, because quite clearly its crisis point coincided with a devastating hailstorm (v.11). We also learn that the battle began just after an all-night march, *not at sunset.* It was the *dawn* that was advancing too quickly for Joshua's liking!

So how do we interpret that interesting verse 13? We are in the hands of the Hebrew scholars here, and I find them helpful. The word for *stand still* can equally well mean 'cease'; for example in 2 Kings 4:6, 'Then the oil stopped flowing' or 'ceased'.

As for the idea of the sun 'going down', it was Professor F.F. Bruce who observed that while the Hebrew word *bo* usually applies to sunset, there is an instance, in a poetic setting, where *bo* ('to come') is parallel to *zarah* **'to rise'**, as in Isaiah 60:1: 'Arise, shine...' (compare Job 31:26). So it is not only possible, but likely, that after the night march, Joshua needed extra hours of darkness to complete his night exercise, and that this was given by means of the massive hailstorm that blotted out everything – sun, moon, the lot.

Is this too far-fetched? Twisting words – in order to avoid some scientific embarrassment! No, this is Bible study. Even the mention, in verse 12, of the geographical position of the sun over Gibeon (in the east) and the moon over Aijalon (in the west) is a firm indication that Joshua's prayer that both sun and moon would 'cease' was uttered in the early morning.

Both sun and moon died on them that day and never put in an appearance at all. It was a miraculous answer to prayer.

16. What is the origin of evil spirits?

Where do evil spirits come from, and how are we to view the unseen world of evil and occultism?

Evil spirits come from the created angelic order (chapter 6). They were not *created* as evil beings, for all of God's creation was good (Genesis 3:1). The Bible indicates that a number of angels, headed by Satan, or Lucifer, rebelled against God's authority and fell (Isaiah 14:12–15; Ezekiel 28:11–19).

The serpent, Satan, is leader of the fallen angels, and opposes himself to God. But evil and good are not co-equal. 'Dualism' (belief in the equal and permanent existence of evil alongside the good) has no place in the Bible. Thus, the translation 'crafty' as applied to Satan (Genesis 3:1 NIV and ESV) is unhelpful. It suggests that the serpent was *created* malevolent. The King James Version 'subtle' (or 'clever', 'talented') is correct. Unlike goodness, evil has a beginning and an end. Satan's final destruction is already assured (Revelation 12:12; 20:10).

The world of the occult (from the Latin: *occultus*, 'secret', 'hidden') about which you ask, is the intrusion into the forbidden territory of **superstition, fortune telling, magic** and **spiritism** (see chapter 69). Its downfall is finally assured through Jesus. His early ministry established a bridgehead against the evil unseen world; hence the hostile, and sometimes violent, reaction of the demons (Mark 1:23–27; 32–34).

Jesus had no fear of demons, and nor need the believer. It is important that Christians avoid becoming obsessed by the unseen world – to the extent that we become either intimidated, or fascinated. After the showing in London of a film, featuring the occult, some 20 cinema viewers went for counselling, under the impression that they had been 'taken over' by evil spirits. They had not. All twenty recovered after a course of prescribed tablets. They had only been victims of suggestion.

We are wise, then, not to imagine, as some do, that every sin, habit, illness or misfortune is due directly to the activity of the Devil and must therefore be 'exorcised'. Terrible damage has been done in this respect by well-meaning but uninformed Christian leaders.

Faced by Christ's authority, the kingdom of spirits has no option but to shrink and retreat. Magic spells and charms have no power over the true Christian (provided we do not open ourselves to their influence), for 'the one who is in you is greater than the one who is in the world' (1 John 4:4). If we resist the devil, he will flee from us (James 4:7). All occultism is to be ruthlessly shunned (eg, Leviticus 19:31; 20:6; 1 Samuel 28 – with 1 Chronicles 10:13 – Isaiah 8:19,20; Acts 19:18–20).

The demonic world is already doomed and defeated (Colossians 2:15; Hebrews 2:14,15). **It is the death of Jesus that has achieved this victory**. We are to be confident, but not complacent – for Satan's kingdom has yet to concede its defeat at the Cross. Its final destruction will be at the return of Christ.

17. What of territorial spirits?

Is it possible that a powerful evil spirit can occupy a city or a country – but that, through prayer and spiritual warfare, we can assist the angels to win?

The emphasis on 'territorial spirits' became highlighted around the mid-1980s, partly through a number of popular writers.

The teaching is based on the belief that Satan has assigned a core of demons to different geo-political areas of the world. This, we are told, necessitates the prayers and fasting of Christian believers, so that we may receive a given 'word' of divine knowledge about the centre of the demonic activity, and thus how to confront it.

First of all, we must recognise that all too easily we can underestimate – or even ignore completely – the works of the devil and his angels. We must always be alert to this (Ephesians 6:10–20).

Is the emphasis on territorial spirits biblical? The teaching certainly *appeals* to Scripture, notably Daniel 10, with its reference to the 'Prince' of Persia and Greece; also Acts 13, where Paul in Cyprus, confronts Elymas the sorcerer; and Matthew 12:29, with its words about 'binding' or tying up the intruding 'strong man'. The deduction is made that if a demon can inhabit a house, it can inhabit a tribe or a city.

Here we must question the logic. The argument is too heavily based upon *experience*. For example, it was claimed, an African tribe only became 'open' to the Gospel when some of its members were 'bussed' out to another locality where, supposedly, the demonic hold upon the area was less strong. Similarly, missionaries, suffering from illnesses and satanic pressure opposing them, would only recover – it was claimed – when flown out of their region. Here are some critical points that need to be made:

1. Too great an attention to formulas, when the Bible doesn't give them. Certainly for many years the Masai people of East Africa seemed impenetrable to the Gospel. But the eventual break-through came, not by a 'bus' ministry, but by sustained intercessory prayer over a considerable period. Thousands of Masai were won, right there in their *own* 'territory'.

2. The neglect of the full message of the Bible. The Bible is all we need. Overmuch attention, given to a few selected passages, raises the risk of serious error. For example, the tendency has been to transfer our adversaries of *the world, the flesh and the devil* into a single camp – that of the devil alone. One possible outcome of dualistic teaching (see chapter 16) is that Christians can develop an obsessive over-blown estimate of the devil and his power.

3. An unbalanced emphasis diverts attention from the real weapons of our faith, the preaching of the Cross. When the New Testament apostles were faced with the entire, heathen continent of Europe, they didn't require a special word of knowledge or superior wisdom (as the Gnostics of old looked for). *They already knew what they had to do.* Look up 1 Corinthians 2:1–5, and you'll see.

18. Were the Magi astrologers?

Over this past Christmas I've heard the wise men, who came to see the infant Jesus, described as astrologers. But I've always understood astrology and divination by the stars to be occult in origin. Can you help?

You are perceptive to have been thinking along these lines. The Scriptures are indeed consistent in their hostility to all occult activity (Isaiah 8:19).

However, we may – in fact we must – investigate those things that God has chosen to *reveal*, and not least in prophecy.

The birth of Jesus – and the star which heralded his birth – was the activity of God himself. *This was nothing to do with horoscopes.* At significant stages of Jesus' life, certain phenomena featured – the dove at his baptism, the light at his transfiguration, the darkness and earthquake at his death, the cloud at his ascension. These occurrences attested Jesus to those who had minds to understand. Similarly then, at his birth, there was a star.

The significance of the wise men – the 'Magi' as they have been termed – is that they were Gentiles, probably from Mesopotamia. They would not have benefited directly from the privileges of Judaism or its Scriptures. It is, however, very likely that they would have taken note of a prophecy that had been uttered centuries earlier – by a Gentile prophet, Balaam by name.

In fact he was from their own area, Pethor, by the river Euphrates (Numbers 22:4,5). His words would have been remembered down the ages:

> I see him, but not now; I behold him, but not near.
> A star will come out of Jacob; a sceptre will rise out of
> Israel (Numbers 24:17).

The star stood for regal power and splendour; the second couplet here is a firm indication of kingship. Further lines point to the widespread rule of this coming individual. Consequently, when a special star came to the attention of the Magi, they decided to investigate further.

1. Their sensitivity to revelation
Traditionally it seems that the Magi (who were a kind of priestly tribe) were to the Persians what the Levites were to Israel; they were respected instructors of the Persian kings. Their enquiring minds predisposed them to recognise and then follow the star, when it appeared.

2. Their persistence in the search
On reaching Jerusalem, the Magi cause great disruption with their enquiry as to where the new king has been born. Herod's advisors look up the prophecies, and announce Bethlehem as the location (Micah 5:2). *But none of them make the journey to Bethlehem.* It is left to these Gentile enquirers to go and pay homage to Israel's king.

3. Their reverence for the infant
Worship – not power – was their aim. Simon Magus (Acts 8:9–11) was in a lower order altogether; through his exploits he wanted to be 'great' – and that is the approach of occultism. Not so, the Magi of Matthew 2. They were wise with the wisdom that seeks God, and were obedient to him.

19. Why doesn't God intervene?

As I look at the violence and persecution of the world today, at the ethnic and sectarian strife, I long for God to intervene. Surely he could put these things right at a single stroke?

Christians, of all people, should be encouraged, because – as Chapter 6 suggests – God's promise to deal with evil follows hard on the heels of the sin of our forebears, Adam and Eve (Genesis 3:15). The woman's future offspring is *a person;* **He** will crush the serpent's head.

'But why not at once?' we ask. The answer is that for God in Christ to right all the wrongs of the human race at a single stroke would mean wiping out the *human race* at a single stroke. Many people long that violence and pain could be banished – but the answer to our question is itself a question: **'How righteous are YOU?** What risk of *you* being wiped out with the rest of the evil-doers, if God was going to end the troubles just like that?'

The Bible teaches that God *is* going to act at a single stroke. In fact it keeps warning us that he will (Zephaniah 1:2,18; Revelation 20:10,14). But when it happens, it will be on a day and at a time known only to him (Matthew 24:36). And it will be the end of the world.

Meanwhile we are presented in the Scriptures with a God of amazing patience, 'not wanting anyone to perish, but everyone to come to repentance' (2 Peter 3:9). No action at a single stroke, then, because of the great numbers of people who would go down under the judgment required to set the balances straight.

So God waits. He works. He agonises. He grieves. He sends messenger after messenger, prophet after prophet. Doctors and aid agencies too. *He's not required to!* But out of love he persists. Many of these emissaries are rejected. It is a pattern of his mission (Hebrews 11:32–38). Finally the Lord comes in the person of Jesus...still working, loving, wooing. He suffers hell's agonies himself, on the Cross.

There is God, the greatest sufferer in the universe.

The Bible teaches us that God has acted, once and for all in Jesus Christ, in dealing with our greatest problem – unforgiven sin. On coming to Christ and his Cross, men and women are forgiven, even of the most hideous anti-social sins, for he has endured the divine judgment in their place, provided they repent and believe. There are many who refuse his offer.

We are still being given time – that is the situation. And while believers can never afford to be complacent, we can certainly be confident, because we know the end result. It is going to happen, as prophesied. If you have a strong view of the future, then be assured that the present will make sense. It is only if we have an inadequate view of the future that the present will seem meaningless.

20. Will the universe implode?

I have read that, just as the universe was about the size of a tabletennis ball when it began, so it will eventually return to the same size at the end of its life. How credible is this?

Let's not be too critical of the scientists; we encourage all those who, like Isaac Newton of old, exercised what he called 'the power of patient thought' in the unravelling of the universe's secrets. Even if the theories keep changing.

But no one will get the end entirely right! Even those of us who read the Scriptures will be dumbfounded at the finish. None of us will nod sagely, and say, *Exactly as I'd predicted.* In our fallenness, we can all too easily get it wrong, despite the clear signposts! Few were ready for the birth at Bethlehem. The disciples were demoralised at the death of Jesus – despite his predictions. The resurrection, when it happened, was a bombshell among them. The Ascension caught them gazing upwards in mystification. The Gift of the Spirit, though predicted, was an amazing surprise.

Thus, when the sixth saving act of Christ – his return at the final triumph – takes place, once again we shall gasp, 'I never thought it would be like that!'

No, there will be no tabletennis balls, but rather *the bending round of the two covers of the Bible to meet each other.* Moses, to whom the first five books of the Bible are attributed, will shake hands with John, the writer of the Revelation. The story will be complete. It will be the same heaven and earth, recognisably so, but completely rejuvenated. The tie-up between Genesis and Revelation – with some 1,600 years separating their writing – is inspired and brilliant.

Genesis records how God created the heavens and the earth; it is the Revelation that portrays the *new* heavens and the *new* earth. In Genesis the various lights of nature are created; the sun, moon and stars; we learn from Revelation that in the new order the only light that we will need will be provided by the glory of God and of the Lamb, Christ.

Genesis at the beginning describes a garden which was lost; the final book of the Bible reveals a restored garden *city*. Genesis speaks of the lying serpent; Revelation tells of the devil's consignment to the lake of burning sulphur. In Genesis the man and woman are running from God; in Revelation 21 the ban is lifted, and God is living with his people.

Genesis shows us the tree of life, denied to the fallen couple by an angel with a flaming sword. In Revelation, those who have their 'robes washed' at the Cross of Christ now *have the right to the tree of life,* and have access to the gates of the city.

We're seeing the video run-down of history in advance. I feel a little like the TV sports announcer as I say, **If you don't want to know the final result, then turn your eyes away from the last page of the Bible!**

Part Two

The truth we believe

Then said the Proconsul, 'I have wild beasts; if thou repent not I will throw thee to them.' But he said, 'Send for them. For repentance from better to worse is not a change permitted to us; but to change from cruelty to righteousness is a noble thing.'

Then said the Pronconsul again, 'If thou dost despise the wild beasts I will make thee to be consumed by fire, if thou repent not'.

And Polycarp answered, 'Thou threatenest the fire that burns for an hour and in a little while is quenched; for thou knowest not of the fire of the judgment to come, and the fire of the eternal punishment, reserved for the ungodly. But why delayest thou? Bring what thou wilt'.

(Bishop of Smyrna, *The Martyrdom of Polycarp*, AD155)

21. Any change after 2,000 years?

Why is it that, after 2,000 years, Christianity seems so powerless to change society?

Let's get it clear – it's not Christianity, but *Christ* who has power to change anything and anybody! Those early apostles believed that the pluralistic world-view that faced them in Europe would give way as they preached Jesus Christ....*and it did.*

Faced by the Gospel, the opponents of the early church failed on four fronts: they couldn't produce a satisfying *interpretation* of life; they couldn't come up with a credible *morality* (their own poets had more morality than the gods); they couldn't testify to a personal *faith* (but rather to superstitious fear); and they couldn't find an answer to *death*. On all four counts, the new Christian preachers had answers that glowed with transforming power.

These followers of Jesus **'out-lived'** their neighbours, in disciplined and joyful living. 'They are forbidden even a lustful look', declared Tertullian in the second century. Hermas, a former slave of the period wrote, 'The Holy Spirit was a *glad* spirit'. But they also **'out-died'** their contemporaries, countless thousands of them being killed in ten mighty persecutions that took place in the first three centuries after Christ. *'It was worth martyrdom'*, observed one historian. Further, they **'out-thought'** their critics; they asked awkward questions about the prevalent superstitions, and subjected the demons to Christ – the highest name. Steadily, across Europe, a new world-view replaced the old. Even Athens' Parthenon became a Christian church, and remained so for a thousand years.

Yet, Christ's humble followers have only very rarely occupied the seats of worldly power. *The reason is that Christ's kingdom is not of this world* (John 18:36). It has no armies, navies or banks. It raises no taxes. It holds no elections. It seeks no government posts. But, wherever its representatives are faithful to the Scripture and live out its message, human experience accords with the statement of the historian T.R. Glover, *The Christian religion stabilises society without sterilising it.*

Go to any country of the world where Christian preaching is outlawed, where the Bible is banned and where another religion is enforced – on pain of death – and see the difference in society! Countless citizens become refugees, anxious to escape the monotonous wasteland created by such 'sterility'. Where do they fly to? Why, invariably to a country where the Gospel was at least once freely preached, and where the beneficial effects are still in evidence.

And that brings me to my last point. Your question assumes that once released into the world, the Gospel's power was automatic in its operation. Not at all. *Every new generation has to rise afresh to the challenge of the Gospel.* The evangelists John and Charles Wesley, at a time of decline, resolved that they were going to change the course of history – and they did. But you and I can't rest on the achievements of the past. **It is up to us to prove the power of Christ for ourselves today. Has he changed you?**

22. The Trinity to other religions?

As a student, I get so frustrated when talking with non-Christian groups at my campus, about the Trinity. Your help, please.

I salute you for the attempt! Don't bother with philosophical arguments, analogies or abstract definitions; they don't help (Isaiah 40:18).

The Bible is your authority. Remember – to most religions – Jesus didn't exist until the middle of history! But if Christ is not present *from the beginning,* then He can hardly be a universal world Saviour. So start with the Old Testament as you present the one living, Trinitarian God who is, in essence, three Persons *throughout the Bible.* Genesis 1:1 has *Elohim* for 'God', a plural noun – but with a singular verb – 'Let **us** make man in **our** image' (Genesis 1:26).

More specifically, focus on Exodus 33. This is the advice of theologian Paul Blackham. Tell your friends the story of Exodus, and of the 'Angel of the Lord' (who is the pre-incarnate Christ – see chapter 23), who accompanies his redeemed people in the pillar of cloud and of fire to Mount Sinai. Moses is summoned up the mountain to meet with someone who is called 'the Lord', but he is also said regularly to meet in a tent at the foot of the mountain with someone equally called 'the Lord', who speaks to him **'face to face, as a man speaks to his friend'** (Exodus 33:11).

Note that, when Moses is up the mountain, and there asks that the Lord, who is hidden in thick darkness, will show him his glory, he receives the reply, **'You cannot see my face, for no one may see me and live'** (Exodus 33:20). There is no contradiction. Moses has no problem with the God who is *one,* and yet who is presented as these two Persons. Nor is there a problem with the fact of *the Holy*

Spirit, who – only two chapters on – is said to equip the people of God, and who is also stated to be 'the Lord' (Exodus 35:30,31; compare chapter 36:1). Other helpful references are Nehemiah 9:20 and Isaiah 63:9–14.

It is a pattern throughout Scripture; there is **the Father** who has never been seen – who lives in the heavens above his people; there is **the Son** who has been seen – and who makes him known (John 1:18) and comes among his people; there is **the Spirit**, who is unseen, yet lives within and equips his people. *The Trinity is basic to our salvation* – for these three Persons in the one Godhead have combined to save us from our sins; in the **will** of the Father, the saving **work** of the Son, and the indwelling **witness** of the Holy Spirit (John 14:16, 23–26; Romans 8:16,17). Try that as a start with your friends.

23. The invisible God appearing?

Is my college teacher right in saying that when God is said to 'speak' or 'appear' to people (eg, Genesis 17:1), it is no more than the naïve anthropomorphism of a primeval culture?

Not at all. Very simply, the 'appearings' of the Lord God in the Old Testament are a pointer to the pre-incarnate second Person of the Trinity. When John writes that Isaiah *saw Jesus' glory* (John 12:41) the reference is to Isaiah chapter 6, where the prophet had exclaimed in terror, 'My eyes have **seen** the King, the Lord Almighty'. *It was Christ that Isaiah saw.*

'No one has ever seen God at any time' (John 1:18). Invariably in the Old Testament, when God *does* appear, and speak with people, it is the pre-incarnate Christ who does so. Nebuchadnezzar sees his three intended victims in the burning furnace – joined by a fourth person (Daniel 3:25); of course it was Christ.

And the Son has these different titles in the Old Testament. Sometimes he is simply the **Lord God** – walking in the cool of the day....making garments of skin for Adam and Eve (Genesis 3:8,21)....shutting the door of the ark (Genesis 7:16). He is manifested to Daniel as the **Son of Man**, a divine being (Daniel 7:13). But he is also **the Word of the Lord**, a Word evidently personified as someone who speaks – for example, to Abraham (Genesis 15:1–6). When we read that Abraham 'believed the Lord', it was Christ he was believing in.

Whenever we read of the Lord 'appearing' to Abraham and 'speaking' to him (Genesis 17:1; 18:1), it is no primitive anthropomorphism. We are reading of Christ. When Jacob wrestles with God in the form of 'a man', he calls the place 'Peniel' (*face of God*), 'because I saw God face to face, and yet my life was spared' (Genesis 32:30). Who was that God who was a man? We know all too well.

In the Old Testament, the visible Lord God is frequently referred to as the **Angel of the Lord** (as distinct from 'angels' or 'an angel') It means *Sent One*. For example, 'the angel of the Lord' is said to declare, 'I brought you up out of Egypt and led you into the land that I swore to give to your forefathers. I said, 'I will never break my covenant with you...'' (Judges 2:1–4). There are similar references in Genesis 16:7,11,13 and Judges 13:21,22.

At the burning bush, Moses meets 'the angel of the Lord', who defines himself as the God of Abraham, Isaac and Jacob (Exodus 3:2,6). This is Christ, who in the New Testament referred to himself many times as '**the one sent** from the Father' (John 6:38). It is this same angel of the Lord who travels with his people in a visible pillar of cloud and fire (Exodus 14:19,20).

It is a consistent picture throughout. It matches the New Testament declaration that Christ 'is the image (Greek: the *ikon)* of the invisible God' (Colossians 1:15). I wonder if that might help your teacher?

24. Where does Jesus fit in?

I can understand God, but I can't see where Jesus fits into the picture.

A theologian called Athanasius, Egyptian by birth and Greek by education, gave the answer to your question sixteen hundred years ago. He said, *The only system of thought into which Jesus Christ will* **fit** *is the one in which* **He** *is the starting point!*

Once we try to begin with our own human-based attempt at understanding God and the meaning of life – let alone the place that Christ occupies – we'll be like the man who tries to do up his shirt buttons, *beginning with the wrong button*. He may hope that it will all work out, and that the shirt will eventually fit properly....but it never will.

So begin with *Christ*, if you want the picture to make sense. He is right there from the start (chapters 22 and 23). All creation finds both its origin and its fulfilment in him, its rightful heir (Colossians 1:15–17). You will notice from Colossians 1:17 that, far from Christ fitting into *our* system, we can only 'fit' – and thus find coherence and meaning – in *his*....or rather, in HIM.

It is through Christ alone that we can know the face of God, and his salvation in our lives. Fully God and fully human, Christ – *the God-Man* – is the perfect mediator. By his saving death he has bridged the gulf between heaven and earth (Philippians 2: 5–11).

No one else will do. That was the blazing conviction of those first-century Christians. Beside Christ there was *no other name* (Acts 4:12). Historically Christ's name claims supreme recognition in all the areas of life that matter most. It happened **in the world of worship** – where the Druids, ju-ju men, witch doctors, temple priests and the gigantic gods Mithras, Serapis, Jupiter and Venus were all swept away.

It also happened **in the world of suffering.** When we put the leaders of history and of thought together, it is quite clear that none of them suffered as Jesus did. In him we see God incarnate, living among us, loving, suffering, dying and reclaiming. This fact alone is enough to explain the beginning of hospitals in our world. *They were never begun by a state department.* They owe their origin to the influence of Christ.

It happened **in the world of creativity.** Christ has inspired symphonies, paintings, soaring architecture and enduring literature. Take Christ away, and the writings of Shakespeare would be meaningless. Atheism, by its very nature could never have this impact, for atheism has no wings.

It happened **in the world of eternity.** The pre-Christian epitaphs say it all: *I was not, I was born, I lived, I am not, that is all.* 'Guesswork is over all', Xenophanes had written. Into that world exploded the message of Christ, bodily raised from death, never to die again. That message alone is enough to change our view of the entire universe. The universe itself only *fits* because of Christ.

25. Should we pray to Mary?

Is it valid to address – and pray to – Mary, as the Mother of God?

Perhaps it is not too surprising that the high regard in which Mary, the mother of Jesus, has always been held, has sometimes caused people to move from esteem to reverence, and from reverence even to prayer and worship.

But the Gospel writers are very careful over Mary. Great restraint is exercised in their references to her. It was possibly during Luke's travels with the apostle Paul, that she confided to the writer of the third Gospel some of the facts surrounding the birth of Jesus.

Is she to be placed on the level of someone to whom people can turn in prayer – perhaps in hope that she would put in a word on their behalf to Christ, to whom she was so close? Let me suggest three reasons that should discourage us from doing so:

1. Praying to Mary contravenes the example of the apostles

The New Testament is teeming with the prayers of God's inspired leaders. In none of them does Mary feature at all. Recall how the apostle Paul prays for his friends at Ephesus – that the Father 'may strengthen you with power through his Spirit in your inner being, so that Christ may dwell in your hearts through faith' (Ephesians 3:14–21). All three Persons of the Trinity are in that prayer – and the fact that Mary does not feature there is consistent with the whole New Testament witness.

2. Praying to Mary contradicts the attitude of Mary herself
Why was Mary selected to be the mother of Jesus? We can readily point to her modesty, her sense of dependence upon the Lord, her obedience and her discretion. On one of the few occasions that her words are recorded, she referred to herself as God's handmaiden or 'servant'. Far from being associated with God's saving actions, Mary identifies with the rest of needy humanity in her words, '...and my spirit rejoices in God *my Saviour*' (Luke 1:47).

Although 'highly favoured' and destined to be called 'blessed' by future generations (Luke 1:28,48), what we know of Mary's character indicates that she would have recoiled from any such extravagant title as 'Mother of God', or any description of her beyond those accorded her in the Scriptures.

3. Praying to Mary undermines the truth of the Incarnation
The whole point of God taking our form and living among us was that in Jesus Christ we were given that vital flesh and blood Mediator between God and humanity. *None other is needed.* Christ is someone we can go to directly, in the knowledge that through Him we have a hearing at the very throne of God (Hebrews 7:25). Our access is immediate, through Christ, the one and only Mediator that we could ever need (1 Timothy 2:5).

We can agree with Article 22 of the Church of England, where prayers to the saints are set aside as something that is *grounded upon no warranty of Scripture.*

26. Is faith a leap in the dark?

The beliefs of my church youth days are over. Can you explain how one could ever be a believer without committing intellectual suicide?

Certainly the problem with some Christians is that, while they advance physically and academically, they never grow up spiritually. They pray the same childhood prayers, they by-pass the burning ethical and social issues; they've never left the Sunday School. You obviously don't wish that.

There are three stages that a believer must go through, if faith is to have any reality. The first is **credulity**, when we trustingly accept what our elders teach us. The second is **criticism**, when we flex our muscles and start to examine our inherited beliefs – even to the point of shelving them, because they have not become our own. But the third and vital stage we must arrive at is **conviction**, when we have come *through* stage two, and – as thinking adults – assembled the evidence, assessed it, and come to a settled and rounded-off world-view that is our own. Until we are at that point, we have not yet grown up (1 Corinthians 3:1; 14:20).

So if I were to say to you, 'Please describe to me your understanding of life on this world – family, work, sex, life-purpose, death, your relationship to the universe' – what would you say? Would your world-view hold together? Could it stand up when the squeeze is on, and life-threatening pressures are bearing down on you? How satisfying and credible is it?

This is hugely important. You are quite right – no one should become a Christian believer at the cost of committing intellectual suicide....*and no one is required to*. True faith can never be a leap in the dark.

What ought to happen is that our minds should catch up with our instincts, as we get older. Our *instincts* will tell us that we are definitely more than blobs of protoplasm wrapped around an appetite. But what does our *intellect* tell us about ourselves, about human love, the world, and life, and God?

Christian faith is simply our response to a given set of data! The *fact* of Christ – how do we account for this fact? It's no good saying that he never existed; for that *would* be a leap in the dark! The words he uttered? *Someone* uttered them, because they stare us in the face out of the printed page – who, then? Whoever uttered them was a giant of civilisation.

Whatever our capacity, we should bend our thinking to the stupendous claims of this man. Certainly, the youth group is far away now. So what, as thinking people, are we reading now? When did we last read the Bible on the *adult* level?

Further, when we are intellectually satisfied that this Man is who he claims to be, we cannot leave it at that. We are then required to ditch our pride and bend our wills to his – as Master of the World, and to say, like Thomas of old, 'My Lord, and *my* God'. That's faith. True, *informed* faith.

FOR FURTHER STUDY: Richard Bewes, *A New Beginning*, Lion Publishing.

27. How does the Cross affect me?

I know that Jesus Christ died 'for' me. But what does that mean?

Someone says, 'Would you go shopping *for me*?' They hope that you will go instead of them. If you don't go, they will have to! It's the principle of **substitution**, or – in the case of the Cross – *'penal substitution'*, as Bible students term it. Someone else has endured sin's penalty in my place. That person has become my substitute.

In football, to send on a substitute sounds like a 'second best'. Not so at the Cross. Nothing that God provides is second best. Jesus Christ, who is God in human form, had no sin of his own; consequently, He was the only person qualified to take upon himself the penalty of separation from God, which is spiritual death (Romans 6:23).

Christ came 'to give his life as a ransom *for* (Greek: 'instead of') many' (Mark 10:45). This principle of substitution is the underlying reality. He died *instead of* me. This works out in different ways:

1. The Cross means penalty paid
The theological word here is *Redemption* (Ephesians 1:7). It's the language of **the slave market**. A price, Christ's 'blood', has been paid for us (1 Peter 1:18,19). Always in Scripture, the word *blood* – when it is separated from the body – refers to death. So, by his death, Christ became 'a curse **for us'**; delivering us from the curse of the law (Galatians 3:13).

2. The Cross means wrath averted
The word now is *Propitiation*. It's the language of **the Temple** – and of sacrificial offering. God's holy antagonism to human rebellion brings us all under judgment. The story

of the Bible is of *God intercepting his own judgment, in the Person of his Son.* The English Standard Version has 'propitiation' as the correct translation in such passages as Romans 3:25 and 1 John 2:2 ('He is the propitiation for our sins'). Propitiation has *God* as its object. We are an offence, and *he* has to be propitiated, appeased; it is *his* wrath that is averted by Christ's substitutionary sacrifice.

3. The Cross means righteousness exchanged

Now the word is *Justification*, and it's the language of **the law courts**. How, despite my sin, can I be treated as though I had never sinned? Only by Christ taking my place at the Cross, and being treated as the sinner – so that *his* righteousness can be freely accredited to *me*. It is an amazing truth completely unique to the Bible (see chapter 29; also Romans 3:21–26).

4. The Cross means relationship restored

Now it's *Reconciliation* – the language of **the family** (Romans 5:9–11). It is illustrated in Jesus' parable of the prodigal son (Luke 15: 11–24). But our reconciliation required that Christ be 'made sin **for us**' (2 Corinthians 5:19–21). Only by the Cross is it possible for us to be adopted back into the family of God as his sons and daughters.

Four wonderful effects of the Cross. The rock principle behind them is 'substitution'.

FOR FURTHER STUDY: John Stott, *The Cross of Christ* (IVP). For the glorious sequel to *The Cross of Christ*, see *Christ's Resurrection,* chapters 50 and 83.

28. What is being 'born again'?

'Born-again Christians' seem to be a special breed – all teeth and smiles. Is it really for us all?

Don't fall for the media caricature! Actually, the 'new birth' is everywhere in the Scriptures (Ezekiel 18:31; 2 Corinthians 5:17, Titus 3:5, 1 Peter 1:3,23). It is in John chapter 3, where Jesus said to Nicodemus, **'No one can see the kingdom of God unless he is born again'** (v.3). Nicodemus had just referred approvingly to Jesus' 'miraculous signs' (v.2), the traditional Jewish belief being that *miracles* would inaugurate God's reign. In effect he was saying, 'It's evident that you're ushering in *the kingdom of God!*'

Jesus, in v.3 implies that – although Nicodemus could see the *miracles*, the basis of his thinking about *the Kingdom* was wrong; no one could 'see' or understand *that*, let alone enter it (v.5), without being 'born again'.

'How can a man be born when he is old?' asks Nicodemus. It wasn't that he didn't understand metaphorical language – after all, he was a top professor! It was rather that he was still trapped in the old Jewish mindset – thinking of God's kingdom in socio-political terms; of the glorious kingdom of David, that had now crumbled under Roman rule. How could such a decaying kingdom *ever* be given a 'new birth'? Nicodemus is saying, in effect, 'You can no more ask for *that* than expect someone to go back into his mother's womb and start life again. It can't be done!'

But Jesus is very firm. 'No one can enter the kingdom of God unless he is born of water and the Spirit' (v.5). Nicodemus can't get it (v.9), and Jesus has to reprove him. After all, Nicodemus is 'Israel's teacher' (v.10); why, he should *know* the ancient Scriptures that prophesied all this! So 'water' here is hardly a reference to Christian baptism –

which had barely been initiated – but rather a reference *back* to those Scriptures that Nicodemus was supposed to be steeped in.

What, then, *were* these Old Testament Scriptures, that prophesied of people being born of water and the Spirit – passages that Nicodemus should have known by heart? The obvious passages are Ezekiel 18:31; 36:24–27; Joel 2:28 and Jeremiah 31:31–34. So, sprinkling with clean water is synonymous with inner cleansing and forgiveness, new hearts and the pouring out of God's Spirit – universally on *all* God's people!

Nicodemus had missed these passages, perhaps concentrating instead on the triumphant 'messianic' passages like Psalm 2.

Make sense of the new birth Scriptures, Jesus is saying. After all, sinful human beings can only breed sinful human beings (v.6)! A new promised generation of the Spirit was coming – a *re*-generation, evidenced not so much by triumphalist *signs*, as by a new morality, new inclinations, a personal *inner* relationship, available for all who repented and trusted in the Lord who died for them (vv.14–16). 'You *must* be born again', says Jesus (v.7). He means you!

FOR FURTHER STUDY: See also chapters 33 and 88. A fuller exposition of John chapter 3 by Professor Don Carson is obtainable on audio cassette from All Souls Tape Library: vestry@allsouls.org.

29. Failure – back to square one?

Having begun as a Christian, I get so dispirited at my same old sins. I keep thinking that I'll have to go back to the beginning again.

No, there's no need to do that. If you are finding it hard, it's a good sign – that you're going with Christ; but that you're now facing opposition!

Learn the unique truth of **Justification**. Once we accept Christ's saving death for us, we are said to be 'justified' in God's sight (Romans 3: 24; 5:1; Titus 3:7). This is a technical word. It features on the computer. 'Justify' flashes up when you want your column of type to *match up* to a single straight norm down the right-hand margin.

It's the same in Bible terminology. How can any of us in the human race *match up*, morally, to 'God's norm', which is perfection, and so be acceptable to him? It's impossible, because sin – which is falling short of God's standards – is universal across the entire human race (Romans 3:9–20).

It is here that the good news of Christ shines at its brightest – in the truth that, despite our sins that deserve judgment and hell, God has himself provided the means by which we can be *declared righteous*. He has come, in the Person of his Son, to bear the penalty of our sins himself at the Cross. By this way alone we can be declared to 'match up' to his righteousness.

Justification, then, is more than forgiveness, acquittal or pardon. If we were simply 'forgiven' (which indeed we are through faith in Christ), there would always still exist the uncertainty of what happens when we sin *again*. But the truth of Justification assures believers that – whatever our character – on account of the Cross, and through faith in Christ, the very righteousness of Jesus has been permanently credited to our name. This is not the same as progressively *making* us righteous (the truth of sanctification – John 17:17; 1 Thessalonians 4:3–7). It's not even that we have been declared *innocent*, and that our file is empty. We have been *declared positively and permanently righteous!* That is Justification.

Certainly all true believers sigh over their sins, and desire to be more like Christ; keeping short accounts with him, and seeking his forgiveness when they fail him. But we don't need to start all over again. Justification stands for ever.

God's grace is its source (Romans 3:24). It all stems from his love, freely given. 'We are justified by grace.'

Christ's death is its means (Romans 5:9). An exchange has taken place (see chapter 24). 'We are justified by blood.'

Our faith is its channel (Romans 5:1). How does it reach *me*? Only as I reach out and thankfully accept in trust what Christ has done for me in his death. 'We are justified by faith.'

God has done it all. No charge can ever be brought against you (Romans 8:33) – it's God himself who has justified you for ever!

FOR FURTHER STUDY: Regarding the truth of 'sanctification' see chapter 93.

30. Does purgatory exist?

What is Purgatory, and how should we think of it?

The teaching that, after death, there is a place or state of temporary punishment before a soul is safely taken into heaven, probably began to emerge around the end of the second century AD. The teaching continued to gain acceptance in many quarters, and was finally agreed upon by the Greek and Latin churches at the Council of Florence in 1439.

The idea – that there is a stage or place of temporary (as contrasted with eternal) punishment in the next life – where souls are purified before they can enter heaven – has been a traditional teaching of the Roman Catholic Church. It gained further ascendancy at the Council of Trent in 1548. According to the teaching, Purgatory is not hell, but rather a place of purifying before heaven; a state supposedly helped by the prayers and Masses offered for that soul by the living church on earth.

But as I understand it, the Bible has good news for believing people. *Purgatory does not exist.*

Advocates for this view have sometimes instanced 1 Corinthians 3:11–15 with its reference to the future fire of testing – but this passage concerns the future *judgment* as it affects Christ's ministers. There is no connection between Bible truth and the notion of Purgatory.

1. Purgatory implies that Christ's sacrifice is imperfect

Are the sins of believers forgiven or not? That is the issue. A look at Romans 3:24, John 5:24, or Hebrews 9:12 fully demontrates the Biblical assurance of sins forgiven. All is achieved *once and for all* by the historic death of Christ (Hebrews 9:25,26).

2. Purgatory implies that God's forgiveness is incomplete

People have always wondered that their sins can really be forgiven. The rediscovery, in the 16th century Reformation in Europe, that believers in Christ are 'justified' and accepted just as they are (see chapter 27) gave the answer. On the Cross, Jesus called out 'It is finished' *(literally, It has been and remains for ever accomplished; John 19:30)*. The penalty of our sins has been paid for, once and for all.

Article 22, at the back of the old English Prayer Book, declares that Purgatory is a 'fond thing, vainly invented, and grounded upon no warranty of Scripture, but rather repugnant to the Word of God'.

3. Purgatory implies that salvation is remote

Naturally, the new believer in Christ feels very incomplete and unready for the next life! But it is *this* life, and not some imaginary in-between period, that is the true preparation for the eternal future.

It is of great assurance to know the three 'tenses' of salvation. 'I *have been* saved from the 'penalty' of sin by a **crucified** Saviour; I *am being* saved from the 'power' of sin by a **living** Saviour; I *will be* saved from the 'presence' of sin by a **coming** Saviour.' *All of our life,* as Christians, is one of Christ's enduring and powerful salvation, from beginning to eternity!

31. Is healing part of salvation?

What is the truth behind healing? Matthew 8:17 states that healings by Jesus fulfilled Isaiah 53: 4: 'He took up our infirmities and carried our diseases'. Does this mean that – as with forgiveness – we can claim healing at the Cross?

At first sight it could look like that. It's been pointed out that the same Hebrew word is used when the suffering servant 'bore' the sin of many (v.14), as when he 'took up' our infirmities (v.4).

However, the same Hebrew word for 'bore' is used when describing those who '*carry* the vessels of the Lord' (Isaiah 52:11). That is different altogether from bearing someone's *sin*. To bear the sin of someone implies that you are bearing its penalty *instead of them*. Can you in that sense bear *someone else's illness*? To atone for someone's sickness is a phrase without meaning.

A clue lies in Matthew 8 itself. That whole wonderful Sabbath evening of compassionate healing took place at *Capernaum* – not at the cross of Calvary, which still lay well ahead. The healings of Matthew 8 illustrate, not the Cross, but *the Incarnation*. God had become human, in true identification with our sorrows. In 'carrying' those pains, Christ was doing so, not as the sacrificial Lamb of God upon the Cross, but as the God-Man, who was participating in our suffering world.

Scripture interprets Scripture. When Psalm 103:3 praises the Lord 'who heals all your diseases', we have to interpret such a phrase in the light of the rest of the Bible (including Psalm 103 itself), where the language used is that of redemption from a *sin-sick* situation, and from the 'pit' of hell (v.4). The same interpretation is given of Isaiah 53:5, 'With his stripes we are healed' – for the apostle Peter connects this verse clearly to our restoration from the ravages of sin (1 Peter 2:24).

On reading the first Christian sermons in the book of Acts, it is quite clear that it was not healing that was on offer, but forgiveness and the gift of the Holy Spirit (Acts 2:38). Healings *did* wonderfully take place – as in Jesus' ministry – but primarily as 'signs' of the rule of God and as pointers to the authenticity of God's messengers.

'Clumps' of miracles seem to mark the beginning of each new phase in God's revelation. The Old Testament spanned about 4,000 years, and some fifty miracles are recorded in its pages – grouped mainly around Moses (and the giving of **the Law**) and around the time of Elijah (and the period of **the prophets**). Next, thirty-seven miracles are recorded under Jesus, and the beginning of **the Gospel**. Naturally there were many more unreported. Finally, ten recorded miracles feature in the book of Acts – with the ushering in of the new era of **the Spirit**. That seems to be the pattern; miracles authenticated God's revelation.

This doesn't rule out healings and miracles at *any* time. Yet even today, reports of miraculous healings tend to come from the frontiers of Christian mission, as divine endorsements of God's pioneer messengers. But more on healing in chapter 78.

32. God as Father? I can't get it.

I could very nearly be a Christian. But, coming from another belief, I have never been able to understand how Christians can think of their God as a father.

Thank you. Although I have read from the teachings of various religions – none of them address God in the name by which Christian worshippers know him best – 'Father'.

1. It is a learnt truth

Get hold of a Bible and look at Luke 11:1–13. Here is Jesus encouraging his disciples to address the almighty, all-seeing God, as *Father* (v.2). It was like a bombshell. Earlier there *had* been a 'Father' term – but used formally, almost as a national title (Isaiah 63:16).

Here is a name that, through Christ, no longer puts the believer at a distance. It is a breathtaking privilege for followers of Jesus to take him at his word and to come to the heavenly Father in the relationship of sons and daughters, in the intimate, poured-out words of our hearts. Fascinatingly even the name *Abba* (similar to our own term 'Dad') is used to address God, both by Jesus and his apostles (Mark 14:36; Galatians 4:6).

2. It is a revealed truth

No one can grasp it by natural perception or religious insight. Go to all the religions of the world and you find that Christ's revelation of God as intimate, loving Father of the believer stands alone. We must go further and say that it is *impossible* to take it in personally until the Spirit of Christ has touched our lives.

If we think that prayer is no more than recitation, then there's still a veil over our understanding. Again, a famous England footballer once said, 'I turn to God when I need him'. *But do we use those we love?* His words betrayed an ignorance of the day-by-day trusting Father-child relationship revealed by Jesus.

3. It is a transforming truth

Jesus drove it home with a humorous little story about a man who, wanting to borrow some bread from his neighbour at midnight, got his way by sheer persistence, despite a locked door and a family asleep in bed (Luke 11:5–13). The whole point was that God is *not* like the man in bed, he is *not* a lender, his door is *never* shut to his believing children, and to him it is *never* midnight. The punch-line was, *'How much more* will your Father in heaven give...!'

The relationship of the heavenly Father to Jesus is on a different level altogether. For this, see Chapters 81 and 83. For the present, if we ask Christ – in our own words – to convince us of this life-changing truth of God as Father....*he will.*

33. What is 'filled with the Holy Spirit'?

How can I know if I am filled with the Holy Spirit?

Certainly Christians are urged in Ephesians 5:18 that they should be filled with the Holy Spirit. All true Christians have the Holy Spirit indwelling their lives from Day One of the New Birth (chapter 28). To have Christ is to have the Spirit (John 14:16–18, Romans 8:9). This is the worldwide democracy of the Spirit!

But there is a difference between those experiences of the Spirit that *began* the Christian life, and those that *continue* it. From the beginning Christians are **born of the Spirit** (John 3:5); **baptised in the Spirit** – in common with all Christians everywhere (1 Corinthians 12:13); **anointed with the Spirit** (2 Corinthians 1:21,22) and **sealed with the Spirit** (for security and Christ's ownership – Ephesians 1:13,14; 4:30). *Once past Pentecost,* the Bible no longer commands a Christian to seek these blessings, for they were already given us when we accepted the Gospel.

But when it comes to Christian *growth and progress,* we are commanded not to 'grieve' the Spirit (Ephesians 4:30); we are to 'walk in' the Spirit (Galatians 5:16); and we are to 'be filled' with the Spirit. This should be a daily, on-going experience, if we want to be useful in the service of Christ. It's a question of *control.* Not (as the New Testament emphasises) to be controlled by wine, but by the Spirit (compare Ephesians 5:18 with Luke 1:15 and Acts 2:15). First, then, *how* are we so filled, and therefore controlled?

There's no technique! First, in daily repentance at the Cross, remove those things that block his fullness in your life. Second, open your life to the Lordship of Christ in daily obedience. As we read God's word and obey it, so he will fill us (compare Ephesians 5:18 with Colossians 3:16). Third, share your blessings with others, in Christian service.

Paradoxically, the way to be filled is to be emptied! Amazingly we feel better and more fulfilled (and therefore filled) *after* a piece of service than before.

How, then, can you know if you are filled? Ask yourself where your concerns lie:

1. Are you more focused on Christ than on the Holy Spirit? It's the Spirit's work to floodlight the person of *Jesus* (John 16:14).

2. Are you more focused on emptying than on filling, and therefore on obedient service?

3. Are you more focused on the moral than on the sensational? The problem with the 'power'-obsessed Corinthian believers was that in moral character they were still like immature babies (1 Corinthians 3:1–3).

4. Are you more focused on others than on yourself? It's always a sign of the Spirit's filling, that we push *others* to the front!

It's a good sign if you can answer those questions with a 'Yes'. And remember, no individual in the New Testament ever claimed publicly to be filled with the Spirit; it was left to *others* to make the observation. So, if someone asks whether you are filled with the Spirit, your reply should be, 'Ask my family; they'll tell you!'

FOR FURTHER STUDY: See also Chapter 88.

34. What is the sin against the Holy Spirit?

What is the blasphemy against the Holy Spirit? Why is it unforgivable? I am very nervous that I may have committed this sin.

It's definitely one of the top questions; it's worried many people, including depressives. But invariably it's the wrong people who worry about it. Let's go to the words of Jesus:

> I tell you the truth, all the sins and blasphemies of men will be forgiven them. But whoever blasphemes against the Holy Spirit will never be forgiven; he is guilty of an eternal sin   (Mark 3:29).

People wonder, What made Jesus say this? But the answer comes in the next sentence: 'He said this because they were saying, **"He has an evil spirit"'**. What is frightening is that it was the religious leaders, who had made the accusation that Jesus, in his casting out of demons, was in league with Satan. They were attributing the works of God to the power of evil. *This revealed their character.*

Jesus doesn't go so far as to say that these teachers of the law were guilty themselves – yet – of such blasphemy. But they were undoubtedly in the danger zone. He shows, first, the suicidal absurdity of Satan casting out Satan (Mark 3:23–26). Secondly, he argues that if He was able to expel demons, it could only be by a superior power to that of the Devil (v.27).

Then, thirdly, He highlights the possibility of individuals who – in the face of the goodness of God, revealed in Christ by the Holy Spirit – wilfully refuse such evidence, and call good evil. What hope have they?

The point is, that it's *the Holy Spirit's work* to illumine people's understanding. Jesus' name for the Spirit was 'the

Spirit of truth' (John 14:16). He went on to say that the Spirit's work was to convict the world of sin, righteousness and judgment (John 16:8). In his next sentence He explained 'sin' in its essence – 'because men do not believe in me' (v.9).

This principle of judgment upon those who have been privileged with the truth – but deliberately stamp on it – is basic Bible teaching. Read John 9:40,41. There can come a point of no return.

This is not rigid legalism, then. It would be a denial of the Gospel of grace to attach a terrifying penalty to an isolated offence. Blasphemy against the Holy Spirit is neither a carelessly–spoken word nor a one-off action. Lifelong blasphemers and fraudsters have known the experience of forgiveness in late life. No, the 'eternal sin' is the outworking of a *character* that stands the truth on its head and treats as diabolical the wonderful things revealed by the Holy Spirit. In such a case there's nothing more to be done. Such are in danger of sinning against the Holy Spirit. *Especially so if they are a teacher of others.*

But this is clearly not your situation. The people who worry about sinning against the Holy Spirit don't need to ask your question. And the people who *should* be asking such a question never do.

35. What is speaking in tongues?

How big a deal is it to speak with unintelligible words and sounds in one's prayers?

Be grateful that praying in this way features in the Bible. After all, it occurs in a number of belief-systems, including Hinduism and even spiritism. We might be puzzled if we knew of no God-given counterpart.

But we do. Admittedly, praying in tongues is not very prominent in the Scriptures. There is the unique instance of the Day of Pentecost, when onlookers heard the Gospel, each in his own language, under the inspired utterances of the apostles. But this is not repeated. Then there are instances, both in the book of Acts, and in 1 Corinthians, when the tongues were unintelligible, unless (as in 1 Corinthians 12 and 14) there was an accompanying gift of interpretation.

Thus, out of the twenty-seven New Testament books, only two make specific mention of this phenomenon (unless you include the textually uncertain ending of Mark's Gospel). There's no evidence that Jesus ever prayed in this way. This is not to downgrade a valid gift intended by the Lord for some, though not for all (1 Corinthians 12: 29,30) – but rather to see it in a proper perspective.

How big a deal? you ask. There's really no big issue about it. If God the Holy Spirit gives to an individual the ability to pray in a special language – so by-passing the usual thinking processes – then it is to be received as a blessing, even though the Bible doesn't define its value, beyond using the word 'helping' or 'edifying'. It goes on to insist that there should be no neglect of praying 'with the mind' also. On the whole, the value of the gift centres largely in its private use. No problem!

Problems only arise when the gift gets pushed aggressively *or* attacked fiercely, in a fellowship. Then divisions can occur. Even a 'tongues movement' can be started! This had become a problem in the Corinthian church. We would probably never have known that the apostle Paul possessed the gift of tongues, had he not felt obliged to correct the unbalanced Corinthians in his statement that he could outdo all of them in regard to tongues – but that he would far prefer to speak intelligibly (14:18,19).

First Corinthians 12–14 is not, then, *the* definitive passage on spiritual gifts, set in a 'neutral' situation. For that, we would need to look at Romans 12: 3–8; Ephesians 4:11–16 and 1 Peter 4:7–11. The passages in 1 Corinthians, by contrast, are given to *correct* an unbalanced church from serious error. Paul's frequent use of the word 'But' deserves study. For example, 'I would like every one of you to speak in tongues [they were doing it anyway], *but* I would rather have you prophesy' (14:5). He uses an exactly similar phrase in regard to his own 'gift' of singleness (1 Corinthians 7:7).

There is no stereotyping. Use the gifts you *have* been given. And give God the glory.

FOR FURTHER STUDY: Billy Graham *The Holy Spirit* (Collins), and the 'Open Home, Open Bible' video series, cassette 4 (enquiries: vestry@allsouls.org).

36. What happens at Communion?

Does a change take place in the bread and the cup during the Holy Communion service? What am I supposed to think, when I partake?

Read 1 Corinthians 11: 17–34, and it will be immediately apparent that we have it in us to wreck even the wonder of the Supper that Christ gave his friends to observe in his memory. *Yet nothing could have been more simple.* 'He took bread...he broke it...."This is my body, which is for you; do this in remembrance of me"...he took the cup...."do this, whenever you drink it, in remembrance of me"' (vv. 24,25).

Jesus never wrote a book. No monument was set up in his name. Instead he left his friends this very simple act of remembrance. The powerful Gospel visual aids of the bread and the cup were to represent his body and his blood given for us in death. In this way, Christ's dying love for us at the Cross was firmly placed for all time right at the centre of the church's memory.

'The Lord's Supper' or 'The Holy Communion' is – as these names imply – an occasion of fellowship, both with the once-crucified and now-risen Lord, and with our fellow-believers. It is a tremendous Gospel occasion.

No physical change takes place in the Communion elements. These outward emblems should never be confused with what they *symbolise* – the body and blood of Jesus Christ. As the Church of England Prayer Book declares, '...the sacramental bread and wine remain still in their very natural substances, and therefore may not be adored (for that were idolatry, to be abhorred of all faithful Christians)'.

What, then, does it mean symbolically, to 'eat the flesh' and 'drink the blood' of Christ? It sounds strange to modern ears. The clue lies in the meaning attached to such phrases in Old Testament Jewish terminology. For example, David the psalmist wrote, 'When my enemies came upon me *to eat up my flesh,* they stumbled and fell' (Psalm 27:2). By that phrase he meant that his enemies would **take advantage** of his downfall. Similarly, he speaks gratefully of those who obtained water for him at great risk. He says, 'Shall I *drink the blood* of the men who went at the risk of their lives?' (2 Samuel 23:17). He meant that he was reluctant to **take advantage** of their sacrifice.

That is exactly how we should interpret this symbolical partaking of Christ's body and blood – **we are taking advantage of his sacrificial death for us.** We come to the Communion, perhaps with a sense of failure and doubt: *Did he die for me? Does he love me? Has he really forgiven me?* Those visible emblems on the table are saying in a powerful way, 'Yes, he did! Yes, he does! Yes, he has!' It is what the theologians call 'dynamic symbolism'. As I receive the bread and drink from the cup, I am feeding upon Christ in my heart, reassured of his saving friendship by the power of those dramatic emblems.

37. What about those who have never heard?

What is the fate of heathen people who have never heard the Gospel?

Too often this question stems out of an inadequate biblical world-view – on three counts:

1. A view of sin that is not deep enough
The question is sometimes asked as though people who have never heard the Good News are in a state of natural innocence – with the assumption that God somehow *owes* it to them that they should be saved. But we mustn't cave in to such dualistic thinking, as though there is a kind of Plan B for 'the heathen'. There is only one plan, for *everybody*.

Does anyone, anyone at all, *deserve* to be accepted by God? No, the whole world is found guilty and condemned. No one has any 'right' to be saved. Across the board we are a race of rebels and an offence to God. Both the enlightened and the unenlightened alike – if they have no faith in Christ – 'are all under sin' (Romans 3:9). But the question can betray something else:

2. A view of Christ that is not big enough
Jesus Christ isn't just another teacher, like Confucius – aspiring to speak across the ages. He is the very Creator, the cosmic Christ who holds the universe together (Colossians 1: 16,17; Hebrews 1:3). He can speak to people's hearts everywhere, and prompt them to seek him (Acts 17:27).

No one, whenever and wherever they lived, is beyond the witness of Christ. Psalm 19:4 says that the heavens 'declare the glory of God' and that 'day after day they pour forth speech'. In the New Testament, the apostle Paul uses those words in the context of *salvation,* identifies them as 'the word of *Christ*' and adds, 'But I ask, Did they not hear? *'Of course they did'* (Romans 10:17,18). No one can claim exemption from personal responsibility before God.

And the power of Christ's saving death straddles all existence, for he is 'the Lamb that was slain from the creation of the world' (Revelation 13:8). If anyone is going to be saved at all, BC or AD, it will only be on account of the Cross, and it will only be through faith in Him who died for the sins of the world – however that message comes to reach them. Let's correct a third misconception:

3. A view of the Gospel that is not urgent enough
It has been argued that those 'who have never heard' will be judged on whether they acted according to their lights. This sounds like salvation by sincerity and good deeds, and a denial of the Gospel. It also cuts the nerve out of missionary activity – which has frequently been an embarrassment to upholders of this view.

But no. The church of Christ has lived by its evangelism (Romans 10:14,15). By the end of the first century AD, there were churches in Europe, China, India and Africa. Had there been no impassioned missionaries to proclaim Christ's good news, *you* would certainly not be reading this page.

FURTHER STUDY: See also chapter 67.

38. Why does God allow suffering?

There is so much suffering in our world. Why does God allow it?

Are we asking the question **theoretically** – as an observer – or **personally** – as a sufferer? *It makes a difference.* When a tower fell, killing eighteen people (Luke 13: 1–5), Jesus explained that the victims were no more 'guilty' than anyone else – but that, unless his questioners repented, they too would one day 'perish' (Greek: be ruined). Jesus was saying, 'Listen, let's stop talking theoretically about *their* death – shall we use this occasion to talk about *yours*?' The fact of suffering ought to teach us humility – one day it will be *our* turn.

Are we asking the question **critically** – as an outsider – or **believingly** – from within the faith of the Bible? *It makes a difference,* because the unbelieving mindset can't account for suffering. By contrast, Christ's disciples, though seriously perplexed, do see adversity as *an intrinsic part of our biblical world-view*. It's built into our framework.

There are four great Bible planks that undergird biblical belief. John Stott helpfully identifies them in *New Issues Facing Christians Today* (Marshall Pickering, 1999, p.39). They are **Creation**, the human **Fall**, God's **Redemption** in Christ, and the final triumphant **Consummation**. Questions relating to every issue in sight may all be realistically faced by reference to one or more of these four mighty planks.

When it comes to suffering, we need all four. *Creation* tells us that suffering was not part of God's original order. The Fall tells us that, by our sin – as custodians of the world – we incurred death and pain, and all that goes with them; even our environment was affected (Genesis 3:17,18). Then *Redemption* tells us that God in Jesus has involved himself in our world, lovingly to reclaim and help us – himself suffering at the Cross. *The Consummation* tells us that, while this process of reclamation is not yet complete, we are heading towards a perfected, rejuvenated universe at the end of this age. This inspires our service towards the suffering world.

Christians can live with these challenges once we understand them. Read Romans 8:18–27 – and you will see how, because of the Fall, **we ache, along with nature** (vv.19–23; compare Isaiah 24:5). We're aching for something better....and it's coming! Thus **we ache from hope** (vv.23–25). The unbelieving world struggles on, *not knowing* there's something better ahead. Christ is our model here, as we find inspiration and courage in *his* sufferings (v.17). Thirdly, **we ache in prayer,** helped by the Holy Spirit (vv.26,27), for sometimes we hardly know what to say (Psalm 77:4).

Ultimately it's only through the Cross, that we can make any sense of our sufferings (1 Peter 4:12,13). We learn the paradox – that suffering and 'glory' run side by side; you cannot have the kingdom without tribulation (1 Peter 5:10; Revelation 1:9). Affliction, then, can lead to spiritual growth and our eventual good (Romans 5:3–5; Acts 14:22). But we only learn this from the inside, and often only in retrospect (Genesis 50: 20).

39. Is everything fixed in advance?

I'm trying to get Predestination worked out. Were my marriage, my becoming a Christian, my job, my clothes all decided before birth?

Advocates of **Determinism** would say 'Yes'; that, although you think you are responsible for your actions, you are only a machine product of genetic inheritance. Such sterile theories make nonsense of morality, and are dismissed in Professor John Wyatt's magnificent book as 'scientific rubbish and spiritual idolatry' (*Matters of Life and Death,* IVP, 1998, p.116). We have only to read of the personal Creator in Psalm 139 to expose the lie.

Certain eastern belief-systems place every event and decision of our lives within the straitjacket of **Fatalism**. If an aeroplane – or a marriage – gets into trouble, this is believed to have been decreed eternally, and must therefore be accepted. Such non-Christian theories deny the God of true relationship, implying that people are no more than puppets.

Recognise in the Bible the distinctions between three great activities of our personal God and Father:

1. 'Predestination' deals with the Christian's destiny

Certainly God predestined the believer from eternity to be 'called', 'justified' and 'glorified' (Romans 8:29, 30) – but without obliterating our freedom to *'come'...* *'receive'....'believe'* (Revelation 22:17; John 1:12; John 5:24). Indeed some passages combine predestination and human free agency in one and the same sentence (John 6:37).

Ultimately predestination is a family secret, recognised only from the inside. We step, by an act of the will, through a gateway placarded by the words, 'Whoever is thirsty, let him come'. We enter – only to look back, and see the caption on the *inside* of the gate, 'Chosen in him before the creation of the world' (Ephesians 1:4). The truth does not lie in between these great affirmations; paradoxically *it rests fully in both extremes*.

2. 'Election' deals with the Christian's salvation

The believer learns with wonder that 'from the beginning God chose you to be saved....' (2 Thessalonians 2:13), and so to be among the 'elect' who will be gathered in to God at the final day (Matthew 24:31).

Naturally it is sometimes asked with anxiety, 'How can I know if I am one of God's elect, chosen for salvation?' The answer is easy. *Christ* is, supremely, *the* Chosen one in whom God delights (Isaiah 42:1; 1 Peter 2:4). So it only needs to be asked, 'Have you come to *Christ*, and therefore are "in" him?' (2 Corinthians 5:17). If so, because you are included in *him*, you – along with him – are 'chosen' (Revelation 17:14). *You are one of the elect.*

3. 'Providence' deals with the Christian's daily life

This truth is not to be confused with Predestination or Election – let alone any notion of fatalism. Rather it concerns our regular care by the heavenly Father. So, while it is your destiny and salvation that are planned from eternity, it is God's providence over your daily welfare that sets you free to work, dress, plan and decide – while still praying in trusting dependence, *Give us this day our daily bread*.

40. Who is the Antichrist?

Can you explain to me about Antichrist? Is this someone who is already here in the world, or is it the Devil?

Antichrist – while not identical to the Devil – is obviously an ally. This opponent of God's rule is named by this title only in the New Testament letters of John.

Anti obviously implies opposition, and so we find the Good News Bible translating *antichristos* as 'the Enemy of Christ'. But *anti* can, in addition, mean 'instead of'; so a second line of Bible teaching holds that 'Antichrist' also refers to an alternative, a *rival* to Christ; falsely purporting to be the true Messiah (1 John 2:22). Antichrist, then, virtually amounts to a Satanic attempt at copying the incarnation – through an evil human personage.

Indeed it is by the *denial* of Jesus, as Christ incarnate, that Antichrist is to be defined: 'Every spirit that acknowledges that Jesus Christ has come in the flesh is from God, but every spirit that does not acknowledge Jesus is not from God. This is the spirit of the antichrist...' (1 John 4:2,3).

Antichrist, while ultimately portrayed as an end-time being, is to be preceded in Christian history by the *many antichrists* (1 John 2:18) who deny Christ in one way or another.

> Some deny his deity, some deny his miracles, some deny his virgin birth, some deny his word, some deny his atoning death, some deny his bodily resurrection, some deny his personal return. Antichrists, the lot of them! (Guy King, *The Fellowship,* Marshalls, 1954)

This Antichrist figure has other titles in Scripture. The apostle Paul writes of **the man of lawlessness** (or 'the man of sin') – as someone who will oppose the Lord, setting himself up in the place of God (2 Thessalonians 2:3,4). The last book of the Bible describes **the beast**, who similarly demands universal worship (Revelation 13:1–8). Jesus predicted the coming of a terrifying demagogue, originally pre-figured in the book of Daniel, known as **the abomination that causes desolation** (Daniel 9:27; Matthew 24:15).

Perhaps the fact that the Antichrist is given these different titles should put us on guard against being diverted by fruitless speculation as to who exactly he is – or against premature anticipation of the End. A knowledge of Christian history – in addition to the teaching of Jesus – should discourage us from such unbalance. *Our main focus should be upon Jesus himself.*

Ours should be the same principle as that adopted in defeating financial forgery – to be so trained in familiarity with *genuine* dollar bills – by their appearance, feel and texture – that the chances are greatly improved of recognising the counterfeits. Similarly, our energies should be focused, not so much upon the person of the Antichrist, but – by training in the Scriptures – upon the *real* Christ! Then, when the antichrists – of whatever kind – appear, we won't have too much trouble spotting them.

Part Three

The Bible we read

I want to know one thing – the way to heaven; how to land safe on that happy shore. God himself has condescended to teach the way. For this very end he came from heaven. He hath written it down in a book.

O give me that book. At any price, give me the book of God. I have it: here is knowledge enough for me.

Let me be 'homo unius libri', a man of one book.

(From a prayer of John Wesley, evangelist, 1703–1791)

41. How did the Bible come to us?

What were the languages that the Bible was written in? And what was the process by which it took its present form?

Broadly, it was Hebrew for the Old Testament, and Greek for the New Testament. As far as the Old Testament was concerned, 'Men spoke from God as they were carried along by the Holy Spirit' (2 Peter 1:21). As for the New Testament, the testimony of Christ's apostles was that theirs were 'words taught by the Spirit' (1 Corinthians 2:13). Here were books, then, inspired by the Spirit of God.

The Bible is a *Library* of sixty-six books, written over a period of 1,500 years, by a wide diversity of inspired writers.

We owe so much to the faithful translators. The first outstanding translation of the Old Testament was the Samaritan (400BC); this Hebrew version was followed in 270BC) by a translation into Greek, carried out by some seventy Greek-speaking Jews at Alexandria (hence its name *The Septuagint*).

It is the Septuagint which, for the most part, gets to be quoted in the New Testament. Prominent among its many manuscripts are two in the British Museum (*Codex Alexandrinus* and *Codex Sinaiticus*), and one in the Vatican in Rome (*Codex Vaticanus*). As far as the New Testament is concerned, there are also numerous manuscripts (see chapter 47).

A mighty translation of the whole Bible (based on the Hebrew of the Old Testament and the Greek of the New Testament) came into being in the fifth century AD, under the hand of Jerome. Intended as a version that all Europe could read in Latin – the common language – this became known as the Vulgate version. It helped to mould the culture of Europe over the next thousand years.

Many have been the scholars. Among them was Baeda (The Venerable Bede, 673–735), born in Durham, whose last dying work was the translation of John's Gospel. And even King Alfred the Great was recognised for his work with the Psalms. Through his influence the Bible was to become the basis of English law.

None of this work was without opposition. After the Norman conquest of England, learning received a setback, and the Latin Bible became largely unintelligible. None was braver than John Wycliffe (1329–1384), who defied the now corrupt Roman church hierarchy – by producing a new translation of the Vulgate into English, so paving the way for the great Reformation a hundred years later.

The Bible in its modern form owes more to the work of the English reformer and scholar William Tyndale (1494–1536) than anyone. Translating afresh from the original languages of Hebrew and Greek, and helped by the invention of the printing press, thousands of newly–translated Bibles were published – in the face of relentless persecution – until Tyndale was finally tracked down at Vilvorde, near Brussels, strangled and burnt at the stake. Out of his work came the Authorised Version of 1611 (the *King James Version*) that shaped the English language for three centuries to come.

Be grateful for your own copy of the Scriptures. It came to you through the blood of many martyrs.

42. Who authorised the Bible?

If it was the church that finally decided which books should be included in the Bible, then isn't the church the top authority?

No; the Bible produced the church, not the church the Bible. This is the issue: What caused a book to be accepted within the 'Canon' of Scripture? (Greek: *kanon*, 'standard' or 'rule'). Regarding the **Old Testament:**

1. Books that were recognised by Jesus Christ as infallible 'Scripture' that could not be broken (Matthew 5:18). In John 10:35 Jesus didn't have to explain what he meant by 'Scripture', though elsewhere He did refer to its different categories (law, prophets, psalms) as pointing to Himself (Luke 24:44; Matthew 24:37). All was to be believed and obeyed.

2. Books that were recognised by God's people because of their impact. God's people will always recognise His voice (John 10:27). Jesus clashed with the Pharisees for *adding* their traditions to the Scripture; yet all were agreed that the Old Testament Scriptures were God's word.

3. Books that were recognised by the New Testament. It is significant that the New Testament features hundreds of Old Testament allusions. Only two are from the body of books known as the Apocrypha (Jude 9,14) – seemingly in similar style to Paul's quotation from a Greek poet (Acts 17:28). The Apocryphal books were perceived to be on a lower level (see chapter 43).

Next, what determined inclusion in the New Testament Canon?
1. Books that are Christ-centred in their emphasis. It was inconceivable to the early church that the Gospels, for

example, which focused so much upon the life and death of Jesus, could have any lower place than that given to the Old Testament Scriptures.

2. Books that are apostolic in their teaching. It was to the apostles exclusively that Jesus promised guidance 'into all truth' through the Holy Spirit's inspiration (John 16:13). The result of this was the New Testament (1 Corinthians 2:12,13). Significantly, Peter brackets Paul's writings with what he calls 'the other *scriptures*' (2 Peter 3:15,16).

3. Books that are faith-building in their effect, and thus, to be read in the congregations (John 20:30,31; 1 Thessalonians 5:27; Colossians 4:16; 1 Peter 2:2; Revelation 1:3). When the Christian Scriptures take hold of the thinking of masses of people, they have the effect of 'stabilising society, without sterilising it' (historian T.R. Glover).

The books of the Old Testament were becoming largely accepted by AD70, those of the New Testament by the end of the second century. The drawing of a line around them discouraged forgers and religious pedlars.

So no one really 'put' the books into the Bible; they put themselves in, because of their innate quality. No council by itself could have conferred authority upon the books; this, they possessed already. *It is an authority that is inherent, not imposed.* If art lovers say of a Renoir painting, 'This is a genuine Renoir', their acclaim in no way invests the painting with authenticity; *it was already authentic.* It is the same with the Scriptures; we can only recognise them as such....and live by them.

43. Is the Apocrypha Scripture?

What place, if any, do the books of the Apocrypha have within the Canon of the Old Testament?

This is really a follow-on from chapter 42, where it is maintained that the books, both of the Old and New Testament, made their own way into the body of accepted Scripture – largely on the basis of the impact they made upon believers across the ages, and because of their consistent testimony to Jesus Christ, God's final 'Word' to the human race.

But what of the Apocrypha? The *Apocrypha* (the word means literally 'hidden things') is a collection of Jewish books that, over the centuries, has not gained general recognition as being on a level with the books of either the Old or New Testaments. It includes such books as *The Wisdom of Solomon, Ecclesiasticus, 3 Esdras, Baruch* and *1* and *2 Maccabees.*

While the Roman Catholic Church did come to consider certain apocryphal books as being part of inspired Scripture, it only finally came to this tendentious and somewhat authoritarian ruling as late as 1546.

Thus, across the vast bulk of Judaeo-Christian history, the apocryphal books have stayed outside the Canon of Scripture. This is not to decry their many worthy utterances. Nevertheless, at the close of the first century AD the Jewish synod of Jamnia took place. Then it was clearly recognised that – while the books of Proverbs, Ecclesiastes, the Song of Solomon and Esther rightly remained as accepted Scripture – there were others that were definitely on a lower level and should not be classed with the canonical books.

The Christian church has taken the same view. Although Jerome's great *Vulgate* translation of the Bible (see chapter

41) included the Apocrypha, Jerome classed these documents in a separate category of their own (*libri ecclesiastici*). To his mind they were useful for edification, but not for the definitive and inspired truth of God. They were different from what he called the *libri canonici* – the canonical books.

A final word concerns the books of what is generally called 'The Apocryphal New Testament'. These take the form of a random assortment of books that, through imaginary reconstruction, attempted for the most part to fill in the gaps – for example in Jesus' infancy years, or in the Pilate story. 'Gospels' are attributed to Peter, Thomas, Paul and Andrew. It is an indication of the high esteem in which Christ's apostles were held, that any number of fanciful documents were attributed to them.

There is a principle to learn from these apocryphal documents, many of which were characterised by various heretical overtones. As Tertullian, at the turn of the second century, put it, **Truth precedes forgery.**

NOTE: Episcopalian and Anglican worshippers are sometimes puzzled by the mention of 'the First and Second Book of Esdras' among the Bible books listed in Article 6 of the Book of Common Prayer. This was only another way of describing the canonical books of Ezra and Nehemiah, that follow one another. All the historic reformed churches are agreed on the content of the Canon.

44. Is the Bible a unique authority?

Why should we believe in the inspiration and authority of the Bible?

The basic answer is 'Give it a try'. See what effect it has upon you by a steady reading of its contents. The evidence for the Bible's divine inspiration will be found within its pages – rather than from external literature. After all, books written about the Bible will all be out-dated within ten or fifteen years. So look within!

1. Its character implies a divine origin

First, **its unity.** The Bible was written over a period of 1,500 years through a multiplicity of different authors. Through types, prophecies, epics, poetry and the hard events of history, the unifying theme of Salvation in Jesus consistently shines through (Luke 24:25–27). Secondly, **its prophecy.** We have only to glance at, for example, Isaiah 7:14, Micah 5:2, Zechariah 9:9 or Psalm 22:16,17 for the point to register. Thirdly, **its purity.** Here is a book that has inspired inventive creativity, self-sacrifice and the highest ethic ever known. Evil is unashamedly described....but so is the answer to evil. Fourthly, **its honesty.** The Bible is not afraid to portray the failings of its characters. It does not try to make super-heroes out of Abraham, Moses, David or the apostle Peter. Nor does it attempt to smooth over difficulties or apparent discrepancies in reporting.

2. Its credentials assume a divine origin

'All Scripture is God-breathed (2 Timothy 3:16)', 'men spoke from God as they were carried along by the Holy Spirit'(2 Peter 1:21). Couple those references to the Old Testament Scriptures with such passages as 1 Corinthians 2:13,16; Revelation 1:1 and 2 Peter 3:15,16 (where Paul's writings are bracketed with 'the other *Scriptures*') – and a consistent picture emerges of both Old and New Testaments presenting at least a claim that their ultimate Author is God the Holy Spirit.

That fact in itself should predispose us to approaching the Bible sympathetically. After all, if I am given poetry to read – and I am told in the preface that this is a book of free verse – I would be mad to open its pages, determined to make the poems ryhme. From the start I would read it as it sets itself out to be. So with the Bible. *Thus says the Lord....The word of the Lord came....God spoke by his servant...*We take note of the fact that Jesus, in his attitude to the Old Testament, **revered it** (Luke 16:17), **believed it** (Matthew 19:4,5; Mark 12:36) and **gave it supreme authority** – *above reason* (Matthew 22:29) and *above tradition* (Mark 7:13). To him, the Scriptures were *the* great corrective (Luke 24:25).

3. Its impact proves a divine origin

This is the practical clincher. There are critics who would say, 'Go on then, *prove* that the Bible is the Word of God'. Our reply to them should be, 'No, *you* prove it. Take it and read it – and see if it doesn't alter your ethics, your mindset and your whole relationship to the universe. See if it doesn't make the person of Christ real to you.'

45. No further word from God?

How far is God still speaking today? Why was the Bible not added to, as time went on?

It's *Christ* who provides the answer to this question. The contention of the Scriptures themselves is that God has nothing definitive to say to us *on top of, or beyond,* his word that culminates in Jesus Christ. Hebrews 1:1,2 expresses it perfectly: 'In the past God spoke to our forefathers through the prophets at many times and in various ways, but in these last days he has spoken to us by his Son.... '

That explains so much. **No one is ever going to improve on Jesus!** After God's disclosures – that reach their goal in Christ and the message of his chosen apostles – we are not going to inherit new teachings that we have never heard before. In Jesus, God has said all that he wants to say to the human race. There is no extra revelation to follow, no additional prophetic word. Jesus himself warned against future claimants to some new messiahship – even if they performed miracles by way of proof; they are not to be received (Matthew 24:23–26; Luke 17:23).

It is not that everything has stood still since the first century! Christ is alive and active, and guiding his church in fulfilling his will and extending the kingdom of God. Hence the excitement and the growing sense of momentum imparted to Christians of every century.

But there is something about the 'givenness' of the Bible that means it is not to be added to. Timothy, the protegé of the apostle Paul, was to *keep the pattern of sound teaching,* and to *guard the good deposit* (2 Timothy 1:13,14). Here is no interesting collection of human insights. Elsewhere we read of *the trustworthy message....the sound doctrine....the faith that was once for all entrusted to the saints* (Titus 1:9; Jude 3).

Quite evidently this is a library of books that is not to be tampered with. Its end perfectly matches its beginning. It starts with the creation; it closes with the *new* creation. It originates in a garden; it terminates in a garden *city*. A tree features in the opening pages of the Bible; the tree of life is present in the final pages. In this way the two covers of the Bible can be bent back on themselves, so that Genesis meets Revelation, and Moses shakes hands with John. How could anyone think of adding extra material to such a perfect entity? This is the book of God and we can only pity those who have fatuously claimed, 'We wrote the Bible; we can *rewrite* the Bible.' As it is, a divine judgment rests on those who would add to, or subtract from, the last book of the Bible (Revelation 22: 18,19).

No, there is nothing more to be revealed....but there is plenty more to *learn*. This is the excitement of Bible study, theology and scholarship. We will never reach the stage when we sense that we have mastered God's book. We need to explore its contents until the end of time!

46. What about the errors?

I get discouraged by people more knowledgeable than I am, who insist that the Bible is full of contradictions. How can I answer them?

'Show me one!' I said to the man who tried the same thing on me. 'Er, well....', he replied, 'How about that bit where it says God helps those that help themselves?' Of course there is no such Bible sentence and I told him so. My friend had another try – and then had to give up.

What do we do with Bible difficulties?

1. Deal with them humbly. Of course it would be too facile altogether to maintain that we encounter *no* difficulties in the Bible. In it, the eternal and infinite God has spoken his mind, and it would be strange if we finite humans found the reading of this Book to be a doddle!

When we encounter Bible difficulties, our first assumption ought to be that there are errors in our fallible understanding, rather than in the infallible Word of God. *Nothing* that God has spoken can be feeble or mistaken! The Holy Spirit is the divine Author of this Book – so, in your private daily reading and study, *ask for the help and illumination of the Holy Spirit.*

2. Deal with them jointly. Others before us have studied the Scriptures and studied them in depth. So, although we are glad of the great principle, restated at the Reformation, that every believer can study the Scriptures for themselves – without the church having to tell them, at every turn, what they are to believe *(the right of private interpretation)* – nevertheless, we do well to consult more experienced students of Scripture. At times we will be like the Ethiopian enquirer of Acts 8:31, who acknowledged his inability to understand '....unless someone explains it to me'.

We can learn one to one...in small study groups...through the regular exposition of the Bible at the church gathering....from Bible commentaries....video seminars with 'Open Home, Open Bible' or the 'Book by Book' video course. Understanding the Bible is not like a private correspondence course, or attending night school! It is a fellowship exercise.

3. Deal with them patiently. It is fascinating how Bible difficulties can melt away – given enough time for us to grow in our understanding. When baffled by an apparent Bible error, it is sometimes best simply to make a note of the difficulty, and then mentally to shelve it for a period – while we continue in study. It may be a year or two later – resulting from our own further reading, or hearing a Bible message – that suddenly the answer to the problem drops into our mind. 'Of course!' It was as though the difficulty had never been there.

FOR FURTHER STUDY: For actual examples of Bible difficulties, see the last section of this book. For details of the video study series 'Open Home, Open Bible' and 'Book by Book', enquire vestry@allsouls.org (for USA enquirers, www.visionvideo.com).

47. Are the Gospels reliable?

I have heard the argument that the Gospel books of the New Testament were tinkered with in early times. Can you comment, and can you suggest a helpful book?

Of course. When we hear a statement questioning the authority of the New Testament Gospels, we are wise to ask its critics for their basis in putting forward such a sweeping theory. We should immediately take them up on a number of specific instances: 'The account of Zacchaeus in Jericho – was that tampered with, can you tell me?' 'The Sermon on the Mount in Matthew 5–7 – how much invention went into that?' 'What about the Lord's Prayer?'

Sometimes people suggest that Jesus never said the things he is reputed to have said. We should push them a little by asking, 'Oh, okay – who *did* say these things that stare us in the face from these documents; sayings that have gone round the world, shaped our vocabulary and brought comfort and strength to millions? Because whoever did say these things was a giant – and I would want to follow *that* person to the end of the world!'

In point of fact it is wonderfully reassuring to the Christian, to know that *there are several thousand Greek manuscripts, containing the whole, or at least part of the New Testament*. Although in the nature of the case we cannot have an original, nevertheless the oldest and most significant of these manuscripts go back to as early as the mid-fourth century AD – an astonishingly early date. In addition there are a considerable number of fragments of much earlier copies still, going back to at least a hundred years earlier.

The evidence is that the New Testament was, for the most part, complete by AD100. For example, Ignatius the martyr quoted from the Gospel of John, and his death is reckoned to have taken place around AD107. The bulk of

New Testament scholarship today dates the writing of the Gospels before AD70 (the year of the destruction of Jerusalem – their argument being that, if they had been written afterwards, such an important event would inevitably have been mirrored in them).

Thus it is clear that the Gospels were in circulation during the lifetime of people who had seen and met with Jesus. As Professor F.F. Bruce commented: 'It can have been by no means so easy as some writers seem to think to invent words and deeds of Jesus in those early years, when so many of his disciples were about, who could remember what had and what had not happened'.

There is every reason for accepting the New Testament documents as reliable.

Again, from F.F. Bruce: 'No classical scholar would listen to an argument that the authenticity of Herodotus or Thucydides is in doubt because the earliest manuscripts of *their* works which are of any use to us are over 1,300 years later than the originals!'

FURTHER READING: F.F. Bruce, *Are the New Testament Documents Reliable?* (IVP).

48. What about the 'later' bits in the Bible?

What of those sections in the Bible that we've later learnt should not have been there at all? How does this affect our view of the authority of the Bible?

First some reassurance. There are such sections, but (a) they are not many, and (b) none of them affect any basic Scripture teaching. They are passages that, on examination by Bible scholars, do not feature in the oldest and most reliable Bible manuscripts. Usually they will have become incorporated later into the main text of Scripture through what is called a copyist error.

There is an example in John's Gospel and chapter 5. Here is an account of the healing of the disabled man at the pool of Bethesda. In any modern version of the Bible you will find that verse 4 is missing from the main body of the passage. It has been taken out of the older King James Version, and has been relegated to a footnote in all modern Bible versions. The now relegated verse 4 reads as follows:

> From time to time an angel of the Lord would come down and stir up the waters. The first one into the pool after each such disturbance would be cured of whatever disease he had.

'That reads rather like a bit of local folklore', I hear you say. And in all probability that is exactly what it was. In fact, when the archaeologists discovered the pool of Bethesda in their excavations of 1876, they found all five 'colonnades' (mentioned in verse 2) and with them a faded fresco showing an angel troubling the water – obviously connected with the legend. The archaeologists also became aware of a subterranean stream which would occasionally bubble up and disturb the pool.

I think we can see what happened. A scribal copyist would have been in the habit of including a little bit of 'commentary' of his own in the margin of the passage that he was copying – not as part of the main manuscript, but simply as an interesting observation. This is what probably happened with the angel legend. Later still, a further scribe inadvertently copied what was originally this margin note into the main text of the passage. There it remained, until – by comparing manuscript with manuscript – Bible scholars were eventually able to unravel what had happened, and straighten out the text. At that point the passage was purified of the extraneous margin note.

There is a similar uncertainty about the last twelve verses of Mark chapter 16. They simply are not found in the oldest manuscripts, and so are now treated as a footnote. **However, far outweighing these considerations, is the wonderfully consistent harmony that characterises the vast bulk of the biblical manuscripts.**

This is part of the adventure and challenge facing lovers of the Bible. It is *because* we believe that what God originally has spoken is to be believed and received as his inspired Word, that every possible care has to be taken to establish the true text.

49. Only 'containing' God's Word?

Is the Bible, in itself, the Word of God, or does it only 'contain' God's Word, as some maintain?

No, the Bible *is* the Word of God. Once we claim that it only 'contains' the Word, then *humans* have taken the place of supreme authority – the assumption being that it is up to *us* to determine what of the Bible is God's Word and what is not! Such a view could be descibed as one of:

1. 'Limited' inerrancy. On this view the Bible is said to be true and without error *on matters of salvation and theology* – but that if it strays into the field of science or history, then it becomes unreliable.

Can you see the flaw in the argument? For example, 'God created the heavens and the earth.' Is that theology or science? It's both! *We can't disentangle the two categories.* Again, 'Christ died for our sins.' Certainly salvation is present in that sentence – but so is history! Once we start to place our own arbitrary limits on God's Word, then it degenerates into the word of humans. But then, in the opposite direction there is:

2. 'Literalistic' inerrancy. At times, readers of the Bible – in a proper submission to the whole of Scripture – mistakenly apply an artificial literalism to every statement. Difficulties occur when we fail to recognise when the language is figurative, visionary or poetic. Confusion can also arise if we insist that twenty-first century standards of computerised precision be applied, for example, to the numbers in the Bible, or to its chronology – *if its human authors were plainly not intending this.* In preference to the above interpretations there is what I will call:

3. 'Original' inerrancy. Our right approach lies in the fundamental principle that has to be applied to *any* document:

A text means what its original author meant.

Question: Did the original authors *intend* – at times – to give round numbers, rather than precise figures? See, for example, the 24,000 who died (Numbers 25:9) as against 23,000 (1 Corinthians 10:8). Presumably the *exact* figure was between the two.

Question: Did the inspired authors *intend* to select the events and persons included in their books? If so, then certain chronological or historical omissions should not concern us – for Bible history is necessarily selective, *interpreted* history – with a specific purpose in view (John 20:30,31). And if Matthew *intended* to highlight the theme of God's kingdom by editing and grouping together a collection of Christ's parables in his thirteenth chapter, then no critic should complain. These are Gospels, not log books!

If a writer intended to give an *approximation* of an Old Testament quotation – no problem! Furthermore, some writers intended only a *summary* of reported speech – or do we imagine that Peter's sermon at Pentecost (Acts 2:14–36) lasted less than three minutes?

Have we got it? The Bible is God's unique, inerrant Word, but we are wise to treat it as a Book presented in *his* style, and not to press its authors into a mould of our own making.

50. Are the actual words inspired?

Are the actual words of the Bible inspired, or only the general sense? I ask because of the differences between the Gospel writers — for example, regarding the resurrection of Jesus.

Well....once we take away the words, there's nothing left! If the Bible is inspired at all, then we must hold to what is called *Verbal Inspiration*.

Let's take those resurrection accounts. Don't be thrown by the little differences. One angel features in Matthew — but two in Luke and John. Presumably Matthew is concentrating on the angel who was speaking. And when did the women visit the empty tomb? 'Just after sunrise', says Mark. 'While it was still dark', writes John.

It was similar at the Battle of Waterloo in 1815. The reports varied *according to your own point on the field*. When did it begin? At ten o'clock, said the Duke of Wellington. At half-past eleven, said General Alava. At twelve, according to Napoleon and Drouet. At one, stated General Ney.

This illustrates the strength of having four Gospels. Some critics seem to insist that they should be identical — in which case they are desiring nothing more than photocopies! In fact all four Gospels *complement* each other. Let's do a harmonisation of Easter Day!

Early on Sunday the resurrection happens. It's marked by an earthquake; an angel descends and rolls away the stone from the tomb (Matthew 28:2). Later to the tomb come Mary Magdalene; Mary the mother of James, and Salome; another group of women follow with the spices. Mary Magdalene arrives first (John 20:1,2); sees that the tomb is open and *immediately* rushes to inform Peter and John.

The *other* Mary, and Salome now reach the tomb, see the angel (Matthew 28:5) and are told to tell the news to the disciples. They go; then, the *further* group of women (including Joanna) approach, see two angelic figures, and are reminded by them that Jesus had predicted his own resurrection (Luke 24:1–7).

Meanwhile, Mary Magdalene has alerted Peter and John, and they set off for the tomb (John 20:3,4), running – with Mary trailing behind. By the time Mary has arrived, Peter and John have already been into the tomb and have gone (John 20:10). Now Mary, on arrival at the tomb, stays weeping (John 20:11). She sees the two angels who ask her why she weeps. She then has the encounter with the risen Lord (John 20:14).

While this is happening the *other* women are seeing the rest of the disciples, but their report is dismissed as nonsense (Luke 24:11). It's probably then, on their way back to the tomb, that Jesus meets them and they worship him (Matthew 28:9).

Some time later that day the risen Christ meets with Peter alone (Luke 24:34; 1 Corinthians 15:5); also with the two travellers to Emmaus (Luke 24:13–35) – and then, later still, with the entire group of the disciples, except Thomas (Luke 24:36–43; John 20:19–25).

If you believe in verbal inspiration, you will do the spade-work of study and harmonisation. If you don't, you won't bother.

51. Can it have different meanings?

I hear so many different interpretations of Bible passages from speakers at Christian meetings. Are they all valid?

No, they are not. If I was to write to you and suggest that we meet next Wednesday at 3 pm 'at the courts', obviously there *could* be more than one meaning to my words. If you didn't know me, you might be wondering, 'Does he mean the *law* courts or the *tennis* courts?'

However, if you knew me even a little bit, or had had the opportunity of reading *other* letters I had written, you would know for sure that it was the tennis courts that I had in mind – no mistake! **In no way would I have dreamt of intending you to make two or more meanings out of my reference to 'the courts'** – that would be the way of madness.

Yet this is the madness of the approach to the Bible made by some modern teachers. They seem to forget that when people write something down for others to read, *one meaning* – and one meaning only – is intended. We hear it said that 'we can no longer talk of the theology of the Bible – only of its theolog*ies*'. It is even claimed that every text of the Bible is 'infinitely interpretable'!

No. **We must remember the principle spelt out in chapter 49 – that a text means what its author meant.** There can only be *one* interpretation of a Bible passage, and it is through study, and a growing knowledge of the rest of Scripture, that we can arrive at the one and only meaning of what we are reading. We are to establish – as John Stott has clearly put it:

The natural meaning – without twisting words.

The original meaning – without bending the author's intention.

The general meaning – without ignoring what the rest of Scripture says.

It's clear from our knowledge of the early church that there was a common acceptance among both apostolic leaders and their hearers of what the Gospel message was. There were plenty of false teachers at hand – but the New Testament letters show total consistency in their combating of error. And if any *alternative* Gospel interpretations surfaced, they would be exposed as 'a different gospel – which is really no gospel at all' (Galatians 1:6,7).

'Whether, then, it was I or they', said Paul of his colleagues, 'this is what we preached, and this is what you believed' (1 Corinthians 15:11). Notice Paul's four pronouns – *I....they....we....you.* There was common acceptance of 'the trustworthy message' (Titus 1:9) among both preachers and hearers! Paul was writing about those things that were 'of first importance' – the death, burial, resurrection and appearances of the risen Christ (vv.3,4). Evidently there was no dissent about the meaning of the Gospel, nor of *the* interpretation. There is no reason at all why that should not remain the case today – at least in those churches that submit themselves to the apostles' teaching.

52. May a Bible story be a legend?

Is it possible that some of the Bible accounts – such as that of Jonah – should be interpreted not as factual narratives but as parables, or even as inspiring fables?

There are some who have held that this could be so. Let me take up your example of Jonah. As far as I can see, such ideas are themselves based on fanciful or biased thinking, rather than on a rigorous application of the questions that need to be asked about a passage. First, *what kind of literature* are we dealing with? Second, *what was the intention* in the mind of the author? Third, *how does the rest of Scripture* interpret the passage?

The parable or legend theory falls down on all three counts. When Luke, in the New Testament, gives us Jesus' parable of the Good Samaritan, it's obvious from the start that it is a parable, despite its use of place names, and despite the fact that Luke never even tells us that this is a parable. *One basic point is made, and there is a punch line* – 'Go and do likewise.' There is no such pattern in Jonah. The story is actually quite involved. It reads like a verbatim report of something that historically took place.

We also note that in 2 Kings 14:25, the prophet is historically *named* as 'Jonah, son of Amittai, the prophet from Gath Hepher' (compare Jonah 1:1). The clincher comes in the New Testament, where Jesus speaks directly of 'the sign of the prophet Jonah', and draws a specific parallel between the experience with the great fish and his own death. He also regarded as factual the repentance of Nineveh's inhabitants. They would be present at the final judgment, he declared (Matthew 12:38–42).

The book of Jonah, then, consists of no fable or parable. The great fish? Of course that has exercised the minds of many critics! But thoughtful readers of the Scriptures were accepting the account as historical long before John Ambrose Wilson catalogued a similar incident, in which the crewman of a whaling vessel was swallowed by a sperm whale off the Falkland Islands in 1927. When the whale was finally killed three days later, the crewman was found inside, still alive. (*Princeton Theological Review,* Volume 25, pages 630–642).

It is not that we *need* the findings of such outside sources to reassure us of the Bible's truth; otherwise the human researchers and archaeologists have themselves moved into the place of supreme authority (see chapter 53). It is essentially the Bible that authenticates and illumines its *own* pages, as we compare Scripture with Scripture.

Many have been the times when critics have dismissed accounts in the New Testament as 'midrash' – as legendary Jewish commentary. But the whole structure, style and simplicity of the Gospel writers dictates that these narratives, too, were a part of time and history.

NOTE: Regarding the book of Jonah, see the six 15-minute programmes available in the 'Book by Book' video series (enquire vestry@allsouls.org; for USA enquirers, www.visionvideo.com).

53. Help from outside the Bible?

How far can a knowledge of outside history, local detail or archaeology fill out and complement my understanding of the Bible?

There have been many Bible students who were magnificent researchers, archaeologists or historians. Among them were Donald Wiseman, E.M. Blaiklock and T.R. Glover. They have thrilled generations of Bible readers with their discoveries. For instance, it is wonderful to visit the site of Capernaum today, and to see the remains of the synagogue that a devout Roman centurion had built for the Jewish locals at the time of Jesus (See Luke 7:1–10).

What is the archaeological confirmation that those lumps of rubble were part of that first-century synagogue? Why, the fact that, onto one of these slabs of stone had been carved two stylised eagles – *the emblem of the Roman tenth legion.* That would have been regarded as an idolatrous symbol to feature on any place of Jewish worship – but for one fact; the synagogue had been provided by the generosity of a member of the Roman military. In this remarkable way he has left his fingerprints for all posterity to see.

The Israeli authorities dug up a first-century Galilean fishing boat in the 1980s. I happened to be in Israel a week later, and was able to see and photograph the boat while it was still at the lakeside. It was 28 feet long. Why, I thought, this just *could* have been the very boat that Jesus was asleep in, during the storm on Lake Galilee. These discoveries excite us.

It is the same with historical research. For years it had been claimed by sceptics that King Belshazzar of Babylon never existed. Surely, they maintained, it was *Nabonidus* who ruled Babylon at that time? But then further research revealed that Belshazzar was made *co-regent* of the country by his father Nabonidus in 556BC, while Nabonidus was away, campaigning in central Arabia; this we learn from the Nabonidus Chronicle.

The great caution about historical and archaeological research is this: in no way can this serve to prop up belief in the truth of the Bible. We do not actually *need* such research to tell us that the Bible is, after all, true! For example, the collapsed walls of Jericho have not yet been discovered. I asked a fine Christian archaeologist in Israel whether this affected his belief in the truth of the account in Joshua 6. 'O, not at all', he answered. 'I believe the story. What we do in such a case is simply hang around. The walls are somewhere in this area. They'll turn up!'

In our study of the Scriptures we are wise, then, not to rely on what is called 'the historical critical method'. **For if we do, then archaeology and historical records have assumed a superior authority over that of the Bible.** Then the tendency is to interpret the Bible through material outside of its pages. No; *we only need the Bible.* It interprets itself. These 'outside helps' are there as useful *illustrations*, no more. They come in the category of what I call 'thrillmanship'.

54. Where is the Bible's power?

If the Bible is the powerful Word of God, why is there not more evidence of that power among us these days?

For a long time there has been – at least in the West – a sapping of confidence in the Scriptures. It began well over a century ago, with the rise of a new theology, particularly from Germany, that approached the Scriptures from a standpoint of disbelief in their authority. It was not long before this negative material drip-fed its way into the universities, the schools, the media and also the church.

We are grateful now for a new breed of theologians who are well equipped to deal with liberal theology – but the damage from the past is still having an effect. In the West, after World War II, the voice of influence was recognised generally as having moved away from the church to the *theatre*. It was there that the serious issues of our civilisation were perceived as being taken up.

It became worse. If the theatre was to become the workshop for today's big themes, much of the church – in its frantic desire to regain a hearing – attempted in an amateur way to play the part of public entertainer! *We have seen a neat exchange of roles*. The biggest-selling tapes at popular Christian conferences have often tended to be those of the speaker with the biggest range of funny stories.

This points to a loss of confidence in the power of the Bible – including among those who publicly embrace it. They do not carry it on their persons, they fail to study it systematically; instead of explaining its meaning in their public utterances, they rely on personalities, music, humour, and marketing techniques, for the hearing that they hope to win.

As a result, the voice of *experience* has gained in ascendancy over that of the Bible, creating two new forms of 'religious existentialism', one European and negative, the other American and positive. Both are equally dogmatic and both are equally destructive. We have to grapple with both.

European existentialism would take as its watchword, **We can't believe that today.** The implication is that what I can *experience*, see and 'prove' is the arbiter of what is to be believed. 'We've never seen a miracle, so miracles do not occur.'

American religious existentialism, which takes a positive form, would have as its watchword, **The Lord has told me....**The implication is that what I feel, sense and experience has a higher authority over all else, including the Bible. If, for example, my religious experiential feelings tell me that it is all right to enter into an extra-marital sexual relationship, they then will dictate my behaviour, notwithstanding the Bible's ban on sex outside marriage.

There is a remedy. The apostle Paul gives it in 1 Corinthians 4:6, **'Do not go beyond what is written.'** We come to the Bible *humbly* – knowing our own fragility of understanding – and *prayerfully* – knowing our own complete dependence upon God the Holy Spirit, who is the Author of this wonderful Book.

55. Is daily Bible reading a must?

I have heard it said that the traditional daily 'Quiet Time' with the Bible and prayer is nowhere sanctioned in Scripture, and is really a piece of evangelical legalism. Is it all right to let it go?

The trouble with holding such a view is that – by the time our neglect of daily Bible reading has taken its toll – our sense of self-perception has dulled and we are unaware that *our spiritual cutting edge is already blunted.*

We then start getting into difficulties over Christian truth, doubts and even about the Bible itself. It then becomes unfashionable to take the Bible to Christian meetings. We can reach the point when a meeting is in progress (even a Bible study) – and no Bible is in sight! The sins that we once had vigorously combated now begin to overcome us – *and we still fail to connect our feeble discipleship with our neglect of the Bible.* But come back to the Bible on a regular basis again – and within days we shall notice the difference!

No, it is not a legally binding duty; daily Bible reading is rather to be seen as a personal daily delight. 'When your words came', said Jeremiah, 'I ate them; they were my joy and my heart's delight' (Jeremiah 15:16). We fall in love with Christ – and we find ourselves *wanting* to read the Scriptures, because they lead us to Him (John 5:39).

Morning or evening? Again, there is no legally binding rule. I've seen people reading the Bible on the London underground. Some find that the evening time, before bed, suits them better than the morning. In a young lively family, Christian parents may frequently lose their chosen time with God because of disturbed nights. Again, when illness – or bereavement – strikes, Bible reading and prayer may well fade out for a period.

For most believers, however, the words of the American expositor Henry Ward Beecher surely apply: **The first hour of waking is the rudder that guides the whole day.**

David the Psalmist knew this. 'I rise before dawn', he exclaimed, 'and cry for help. I have put my hope in your word' (Psalm 119:147). This sounds like a habit!

Isaiah knew it too. 'The sovereign Lord has given me an instructed tongue, to know the word that sustains the weary. He wakens me morning by morning, wakens my ear to listen like one being taught' (Isaiah 50:4).

That sounds to me like *every day*! The apostle Peter exhorted his readers to receive God's 'pure spiritual milk', so that by it they might 'grow up' in their salvation. He then goes on to say, 'As you *come* to him, the living Stone....' and the Greek of the text indicates that they were to *continue* coming, in this way (1 Peter 2:2–4).

Let daily Bible reading and prayer be like the meeting of lovers for an agreed appointment. As Søren Kierkegaard of Denmark once observed, *A believer is surely a lover; yea, of all lovers the most in love!*

FOR FURTHER STUDY: Read Chapter 77.

56. The Bible – and listening to God?

I'm told that I must spend time listening to God. But how can I know that it is His voice I'm hearing?

You have hit on a desperately important issue. Throughout history there are those who have claimed that, as they passively 'listened' God spoke to them – and then all too often have performed irrational actions on the basis of what proved to be a delusion. It sounds mystical, even a little super-spiritual, to say that I have heard the voice of God. But it is only a self-authenticating claim. *Where is the independent check that this is so?*

Among the very worst examples were the events that led to the ill-fated Christian 'Crusades' of the Middle Ages. What madness prompted Pope Urban II to fly in the face of Christ's commands, by calling for military action against the Muslims – in a sermon at Clermont in 1095? The crowd's shouted response, 'God wills it!' became the slogan that spread shame upon the face of Christ's mission of love to the world.

God wills it....God spoke to me. How many times such sentiments have been used, publicly and privately, to sanction unfortunate projects and programmes, unwise liaisons and empty-headed schemes that – if only the Scriptures had been heeded – could have been avoided?

We *should* listen to God – and the sure and certain way to do it is to come to Him in humility with the Bible opened before us. As we prayerfully take in what we are reading, we may expect God's Holy Spirit to apply the words, and to prompt us, here and now! I do not read in Hebrews 3:7 that centuries ago someone imparted a warning to people who lived a long time ago. I read, 'So, as the Holy Spirit **says, "Today, if you will hear his voice,** do not harden your hearts"'. I read God's Book – and I become aware, 'He's speaking to *me*!'

Look up Ephesians 4:21. The modern versions translate it, 'Surely you heard *of* him' (Christ). But the King James Version has it correct, for the word 'of' is not present in the Greek text. The true translation then is 'Surely you heard *him'*.

'Really?' we question. 'But those Ephesian Christians were far from the land where Jesus lived and taught. They only heard Paul and his friends!'

Not so. They were listening to preachers, *but they had also become aware that another voice had taken over.* They heard Jesus!

It happens today. Countless are the times when people, at the end of a sermon or Bible study exclaim, 'That was for me; Jesus was speaking to *me*!'

If you really believe that the Lord speaks to us through the Scriptures – applying them by His Spirit personally and practically – we will take the Bible more seriously. Do you carry it into every day with you? In your pocket, handbag or briefcase? Small pocket Bibles can be expensive....but why not put one on your birthday or Christmas list? And do a great deal more reading, and therefore plenty of listening!

FOR FURTHER STUDY: Video programme: Cassette 1, programme 4 of the 'Open Home, Open Bible Series' features Joni Eareckson Tada, speaking with Paul Blackham and Richard Bewes on this important topic.

57. Should the Bible be banned?

I read in a newspaper that someone was trying to obtain a court ruling that the Bible is an obscene book. What is the Christian answer?

Opponents of Jesus Christ will go on trying to ban the Bible until the end of time; we should not be surprised or alarmed. Any pretext will do!

The notorious Ugandan president, Idi Amin, declared in his time that the word *Israel* ought to be deleted, throughout the Bible, on the grounds that it was a racist book. A prominent homosexual campaigner once admitted that in any hotel bedroom containing a Gideon Bible, he would tear out the pages where homosexual activity is condemned.

About the case that you instance, there are bound to be individuals who poke around in the Scriptures, trying to discover passages about immoral deeds. But we should ask the critic whether he had ever been into a pornographer's shop, and if so, how many Bibles had been on display.

Society in the end is likely to side with the historian G.M. Trevelyan. He wrote of the seventeenth century that the effect of the study of the Bible *'upon the national character, imagination and intelligence for nearly three centuries to come was greater than that of any literary movement in our annals or any religious movement since the coming of St Augustine'*.

Certainly, there are Bible passages that – if they were read in public – would make us wriggle with unease. They deal with the category of life that the apostle Paul described as 'fruitless deeds' that were 'shameful even to mention' (Ephesians 5:12). The same could be said of what are sometimes called the *imprecatory psalms*, which include such very human sentiments as 'Break the teeth in their mouths, O God!'

We should not think that such passages are any less 'inspired', or less pure than the rest of God's Word. They all form part of the total inspired revelation – a revelation which puts its entire weight behind goodness and purity. The 'impure' events related in its pages are there as part of the realistic picture given us of fallen, unredeemed humanity.

Would we have wanted the Bible in another guise; sweetly 'religious', varnished and sanitised by church-approved phraseology?

Maybe the campaigner you mention hasn't stopped to think that if the Bible did indeed become a banned book, most of the world's famous literature would die with it – Dostoevsky, Tolstoy, Milton, Bunyan and Walter Scott....book after book. There are 300 Bible quotations in Tennyson's works alone. There are over 500 biblical allusions in the writings of Shakespeare. Even Karl Marx's *Das Kapital* would have to be changed, along with his other writings, if the Bible disappeared. At a stroke, the artistic works of Michelangelo, Raphael and Leonardo da Vinci would be reduced to unintelligibility, together with the great music of the world – Beethoven, Mozart and Handel.

The apostle Paul, chained like a criminal in prison, wrote 'But God's word is not chained' (2 Timothy 2:9). And it never can be. Nor permanently.

58. Nothing but the Bible?

Is it best if my Christian reading is confined to the reading of the Bible alone?

If your question implies what I think it does – that at heart you want to be, as John Wesley once expressed it, a person 'of one book' – then I want to affirm you strongly. In your own times of quiet with the Lord, let it be the Bible that you focus on exclusively. We need our spirits to be fed by the 'pure spiritual milk' (1 Peter 2:2), rather than by derivative, secondary material; by the Bible *itself*, rather than by *echoes* of the Bible.

This does not rule out using helpful Bible notes or commentaries for daily reading – provided that the writers of these aids are consistently pointing the reader back to Scripture all the time, rather than to their own thoughts or clever ideas.

And let it be the Bible, clear and simple. Some Bible students have a marked Bible. In the margin, they may write down some of their findings; they may use highlighters to mark what they consider to be especially helpful. It's fine to do this, but my strong recommendation is that we should never use such a marked Bible *for our daily devotional reading* because the tendency then will be for our eyes to be drawn away from the text to those human elements that have been added. We need to come to the pages of the Bible freshly each time – as though we had never seen them before!

But now let us make another point. The Baptist preacher C.H. Spurgeon once commented on Paul's request for books, in a sermon on 2 Timothy 4:13: **'Even an apostle must read. He's inspired, yet he wants books! He has seen the Lord and yet he wants books! He's been caught up to the third heaven, yet he wants books!'** This tells us that there is every reason – in our growth as mature, thinking believers – for the acquiring of Christian books, and for the setting apart of extra time for reading and study.

Even as busy a man as King Alfred the Great did this. Back in the ninth century he was the first truly great Christian king of England. He put himself and his courtiers through school. He would set apart eight hours for sleep, meals and recreation, eight for public duties, and eight for reading, study and prayer.

The reasoning is this; if top scholars have given the best part of their lives to the understanding of God's Word, then we should be glad to benefit from the fruit of their studies. Commentaries on the Bible itself, books on Christian teaching and ethics, books on how to share our faith with others, books that help us deal with modern controversies and other religions; Christian biographies, church history and missionary thrillers....all of these are going to *help*.

Go to your own church bookstall, or to reliable Bible bookstores, and see if you can't build up your own Christian library.

59. What about 'atrocities' in the Bible?

I have heard it said that Moses was no better than Molosovic, in the slaughters that we read about in the Old Testament. Is the morality different between the Old and New Testaments?

No, it is exactly the same. The problem with some people is that they would like it both ways, when it comes to God's morality. Sometimes they will complain, 'Why can't God *deal* with the perpetrators of such acts as September 11, 2001 – at a single stroke?' At other times they will be heard to say, 'Look at the apalling way in which God dealt with the Amorites and wiped them out at a stroke!'

If retribution for human wickedness is delayed, it is because of God's patience – but it is certain to come. In the words of Von Logau's poem *Retribution* – translated by the American poet Longfellow –

> Though the mills of God grind slowly,
>   yet they grind exceeding small.

That is exactly it. Second Peter 3:3–9 refers to both the Flood of Noah and the fire of the final Day *in making the same point;* that God is not slow in bringing retribution upon wickedness; it will take place. At the same time He is 'patient....not wanting anyone to perish, but everyone to come to repentance' (2 Peter 3:9).

At the time of the Flood the Lord declares, 'My Spirit will not contend with man for ever' (Genesis 6:3). We learn of the 'grief' and 'pain' of God over sinful humanity. Retribution was universal – but so was the message of saving grace that then fanned out from Noah's family to the developing nations.

The Amorites in their day were notorious for their child sacrifice and unprincipled living. Why were they not wiped out forthwith? But it is explained to Abraham that 'the sin of the Amorites has not yet reached its full measure' (Genesis 15:16). Hundreds of years passed in which the long-suffering Lord waited for the Amorites, before his terrible vengeance overtook them (Numbers 21).

The principle of these judgments is the recognition on a public scale – for all to see – that wickedness will be overthrown. Even Israel is not exempt. If necessary, God would use a heathen nation to bring judgment upon His own people. **Yet the fearful judgments of history were but warning pointers to the most terrible fate of all – banishment for all eternity to the hell of final separation from God.**

The judgments of the Bible provide humanity with an *Education*; sin will always meet its deserts. They also give *Comfort* to all who long for justice. They also impart a *Warning* – as we look back to the past (1 Corinthians 10:11), and as we look forward to the end time (2 Peter 3:11,12). Be glad that the Lord does not ignore wickedness. **Be thankful too that, to spare us from final judgment, He endured the worst 'atrocity' of all – the Cross, where the sinless Christ underwent the agony of the retribution that should have been ours.**

60. The Bible – a selection process?

I am aware of a kind of 'selection' process running throughout the whole Bible. But who gets the blessing, and on what basis? Is it fair?

You are basically asking, 'Who are the children of Abraham, the "father of all believers"'? Jews claim Abraham on the basis of the genetic line through Isaac; Muslims on the strength of the line through Ishmael.

But these claims – and others like them – are untrue to the Bible. God's selection for blessing is simply not based on genetics – otherwise the rejected Esau could stake as good a claim as anyone. We are not to think of this as an ethnic, racial or cultural issue (for then it *would* be unfair), but as one involving *faith*.

See the 'shape' of the Bible like that of an old-fashioned sandglass, with which people used to time the boiling of their eggs – wide at each end, and narrow in the middle.

At the 'top end' of the Bible, the scale is massive: 'Let us make man in our own image' – and our human story begins. But then we trace a narrowing-down process, as God selects the human instruments by which His love will be made known to the world – and the Old Testament takes up the story of Abraham, and a single family and nation – the people of Israel.

It narrows down further, as four-fifths of the nation goes into captivity, owing to Israel's failure to be a faithful light to the world, and we're left with Judea – a tiny kingdom, no bigger than Yorkshire or New Jersey.

It gets smaller still, because even that little company gets carried off into captivity – and although the exiles eventually return, it looks as though Israel's light has gone out, with the Persians, Greeks and finally the Romans occupying the world stage. There is just a small 'remnant' of faithful ones at the end of the Old Testament.

Four hundred years pass, and we enter the New Testament, and the sandglass has narrowed down to thirteen individuals. Surely it couldn't get any smaller – but it does. The drama boils to a crisis, one member turning traitor, another turning coward; the rest scattering....and we're left, at the narrowest point of the sandglass, with the *one Figure* of Jesus – who dies in solitary degradation.

And everything in the divine kingdom and plan hangs upon His faithful sacrifice and death. At that point *He* is 'Israel'; *He* is the chosen people; *He* is the faithful fulfilment of the age-long Covenant. One Person!

From then on, a broadening process begins, as the message of love and forgiveness – centring in Christ – travels out in ever widening circles, Jerusalem, Judea, Samaria....and the ends of the earth (Acts 1:8).

Christ is **the** chosen one (Isaiah 42:1; 1 Peter 2:4). As men and women of every ethnic background and culture put their *faith* in Him, they too may be said to be 'chosen in Him' (Ephesians 1:4), and to be true children of Abraham. That is the story of the Bible.

Part Four

The way we behave

We recognise a tree by its fruit; and we ought to be able to recognise Christians by their actions. The fruit of faith should be evident in our lives, for being a Christian is more than a matter of making sound professions of faith. It should reveal itself in practical and visible ways.

Indeed, it is better to keep quiet about our beliefs, and live them out; than to talk eloquently about what we believe, but fail to live by it.

(Ignatius of Antioch, c. AD35–107)

61. Is Christianity the highest ethic?

It seems to me that all the different religions have something to offer. How can Christianity lay claim to providing the highest ethic?

The answer has to be, *Look at the Founder.* We must stress that right away, because 'religions' – as historical movements – can too easily compromise the ideals of their founders – either through deterioration and distortion; or by deliberate camouflage, as character defects become revealed about their leaders – often from their own records. Always we must go back to the original prototype, and ask, 'Can *this* figure credibly lay claim to being the all-time Teacher of the world?

In such a quest, character is absolutely vital. For a teacher of physics, or a football coach, character is not seen to be the biggest issue. They may have a range of dubious sexual relationships, or have a violent temper, but, provided they are reasonable citizens, it is their professional ability that is under scrutiny.

Not so, when it comes to aspirants for the role of light-bearer for all humanity. Their character, more than all else, must come under the microscope. It is not the slightest good to advance their claim if they have a scant regard for human life, if they have an assortment of wives and dubious relationships, if they are piling up money or if they fail to become personally involved in the suffering world around them.

You mention Christianity. There have been plenty of deviations from the original prototype – particularly by those who have found it profitable to operate under Christ's banner while forming their own power base, whether materialist, militarist or racist. Some religious practitioners will call Jesus 'Lord' – only to be told by Him at the last judgment 'I never knew you. Away from me, you evil-doers!' (Matthew 7:23).

So, back to the prototype. It's here that I become convinced of the validity of Christ's claim to be 'the way, the truth and the life' (John 14:6). Other religious leaders would say, 'I have discovered the answer; now follow this teaching.' But none of them claimed to *be* the answer, as Jesus did. And none of them said, as Jesus did, 'Follow *me*'.

It is the intrinsic, magnetic *goodness* of Jesus that has drawn millions of us – unattractive characters as many of us are – to His feet. Unlike some leaders, He has not won our loyalty by temporal inducements or by force of arms. He has a totally unblemished record in the area of intimate human relationships. He betrays no hint of a remote 'other-world' detachment from human calamity. The beginning of hospitals and the care of leprosy sufferers – whom other groups never dared touch – derive from Him. The lifting of oppression from women in society – although long resisted, even today – is due to Christ. And *the* behavioural feature that marks out the true Christian – love of one's enemy – we owe to Jesus.

It was well said by the fourth-century Christian leader, Ephraem of Syria, 'There never was a King like this before!'

62. How dangerous is wealth?

What are the moral issues surrounding the topic of wealth creation?

First of all we should recognise that Christianity doesn't present us with a biblical economic theory. Rather, it gives us a viewpoint, a perspective on *life,* that helps us to cope with money and to manage it. Here is an example:

> Command those who are rich in this present world not to be arrogant nor to put their hope in wealth, which is so uncertain, but to put their hope in God, who richly provides us with everything for our enjoyment. Command them to do good, to be rich in good deeds, and to be generous and willing to share (1 Timothy 6:17–19).

Clearly, although there is a great danger attached to riches, and although the believer is to show a true solidarity with the poor, there is nothing intrinsically wrong with wealth in itself. And poverty is not an indispensable mark of the believer. It is not God's will that poverty should be the rule of life across the world.

However, 'Wealth is like a viper', said Clement of Alexandria at the turn of the second century. Richard Foster of our own time gets close to this opinion, with his claim that money has a spiritual, even a demonic character of its own (*Money, Sex and Power*, Hodder and Stoughton). Perhaps this view fails to take into account the difference between 'money' and 'mammon' – which is the love of money and its virtual personification (see Luke 16:11 KJV and 1 Timothy 6:10).

The debate about wealth creation has been a long one. Max Weber in *The Protestant Ethic and the Spread of Capitalism* (1904) maintained that the biblical outlook of

Protestantism enabled a person 'to see in his ordinary daily work an activity pleasing to God and therefore to be pursued as actively and profitably as possible'. Weber maintained that the ethos of Protestantism promoted, as nothing else could have done, the spirit of the entrepreneur, and for that reason wealth creation was to be found largely in countries with a biblical heritage.

Weber was challenged by R.H. Tawney in *Religion and the Rise of Capitalism* (1926). While Weber saw wealth creation as one of the positive results of the Protestant view, Tawney attacked not only capitalism for its failure to provide social justice, but also Protestantism for perverting the Christian message of poverty and charity into a gospel of 'success'.

Tawney was not entirely right. For it is obvious that Luther and Calvin, to take two earlier Protestant leaders, disapproved of profit-making as something worthy in itself. The characteristic emphasis of all early Protestant teaching about wealth was moralistic – with the stress on charity, rather than self-advancement. As John Wesley was to advise in the eighteenth century, 'Make all you can, save all you can, *give all you can.*'

All too easily, of course, a productive, biblical world-view can become eroded by the Fall – *then mammon takes over*. Conversely, when wealth has come into the hands of true Christians, the benefits are wide-ranging indeed.

63. What is meant by 'spirituality'?

People say things like, 'What are you doing about Spirituality at your church these days?' What is really meant by this term?

In 1883 the top blew off the volcanic island of Krakatoa in Indonesia. The explosion was heard 3,000 miles away, and the tidal waves reached Cape Horn, 8,000 miles distant. It was the most stupendous explosion ever recorded in history.

Krakatoa is a kind of spiritual parallel to what happened in our world through the death and resurrection of Jesus Christ. The great difference is that, while Krakatoa was destructive, the Cross – and subsequent Resurrection – created the greatest ever shock-wave of hope and confidence. Its tidal waves are still being felt, everywhere. It is the 'epicentre' of all Christian experience.

And Christian experience matches with the term 'Spirituality'. Wakefield's *Dictionary of Christian Spirituality* describes it as 'those attitudes, beliefs and practices which animate people's lives and help them to reach out towards super-sensible realities'.

I tend to use the term 'Christian growth' rather than 'Spirituality', for we are considering those influences that *centre and develop us* in the life of Christ – once crucified, but raised to the right hand of power. The grace of **God** is our foundation; the death of **Christ** is our centre, and the everyday relationship with the living Christ by His **Spirit** is our dynamic. Yes, effective Christian living is essentially Trinitarian.

The problem with some spiritualities is that they focus on *ourselves*. The worship hymns that are chosen make it obvious. Too many of them contain echoes of the Bible, but their main theme seems to be 'Aren't we wonderful?'! It is the same with certain disciplines and observances that can create a self-obsessed illusion of mystical 'holiness', without actually dealing with our sinful characters.

Colossians 2:16 – 3:17 is a useful passage. See if you can spot the four 'with Christ's of 2:20, 3:1; 3:3 and 3:4 – and work on them! In this chapter, the apostle Paul condemns the rituals and mystical experiences that caused people to *lose connection with Christ the Head* (2:19) – impressive-looking religious disciplines that were nevertheless 'based on human commands and teachings'. The implication is that you can be only one degree off course, but – such is the principle of the angle – in ten years' time you will be far from your epicentre, and never know it.

At base, there is the Christian fellowship (3:12–15) and 'the word of Christ' (3:16) to protect and build us. Elsewhere we learn of intercession and the coming together of the fellowship for the Lord's Supper.

From my childhood, ours was a spirituality built on Bible stories, daily meditation on the Scriptures, the Christian family (and family prayers), the reading of books, prayer meetings, the missionary imperative and, as we found in East Africa, suffering. It is beyond me to understand why, in numerous books on 'Spirituality', this last ingredient is conspicuously missing. Acts 14:22 and elsewhere tell us that it is *essential* (see chapter 38). We are, after all, following the way of the Cross.

64. What about forgiving the unrepentant?

Is it biblical to forgive those who show no remorse for their actions?

It is the love of one's enemies which distinguishes the true disciple of Jesus Christ. In Burundi, at the height of its violent troubles, an African Christian was facing the guns of his enemies. 'Before you kill me', he said, 'may I have permission to say a few things?'
– 'Say it quickly.'
– 'First,' he said, 'I love you. Second, I love my country. Third, I will sing a song.' In their mother tongue, he then sang all four verses of the hymn which begins, *Out of my bondage, sorrow and night; Jesus I come, Jesus I come'*. And then the shots rang out. This African Christian was simply following the example of his Leader, in the saying from the Cross which has stamped itself upon the world's consciousness, 'Father, forgive them, for they do not know what they are doing' (Luke 23:34). The words were to be echoed by Stephen (Acts 7:60) – the first of a long and honourable procession of martyrs.

Such attitudes are the outworking of the Lord's teaching in the Sermon on the Mount: 'Love your enemies and pray for those who persecute you' (Matthew 5:44).

The New Testament emphasis, then, is on the *attitude* that leans out towards one's persecutors. A minister friend of mine spoke movingly on television from his hospital bed, after being attacked by intruders in his own house. He explained that he felt no resentment towards those men.

But given all this, your question raises the acute issue of how far forgiveness can be practically given to those who exhibit no repentance. All too often someone who has been on the receiving end of an attack is then asked by media people – or perhaps by the unthinking – *Have you forgiven them?*

Put just like that, it is a shallow question. It also places an additional burden on, say, the rape victim who is then advised, 'You cannot recover until you have forgiven your attacker'. Ironically it is the rape victim who is unfairly placed in the dock.

Jesus' words help us: 'If your brother sins, rebuke him, and if he repents, forgive him' (Luke 17:3). Commenting on this passage, John Stott adds – 'and only if he repents. We must beware of cheapening forgiveness....If a brother who has sinned against us refuses to repent, we should not forgive him. Does this startle you? It is what Jesus taught' (*Confess your Sins*, Hodder, 1964, p.35).

The reason is that real forgiveness implies restoration to full fellowship. This cannot be if the sinner is unrepentant. As John Stott observes, 'A forgiveness, which bypasses the need for repentance, issues not from love but from sentimentality'.

The attitude of being *willing* to forgive (or even being willing to be made willing) is in itself costly. It comes from the Cross itself, where a Man died for our own forgiveness. Realise that – and a revolution of love can take place.

65. Can euthanasia be Christian?

Is it not only humane, but compassionately Christian, to follow the Dutch medical trend towards assisting in the termination of a life not worth living?

The division between right and wrong can look paper-thin, even blurred, when isolated and emotional cases are cited. But if you saw someone high on a parapet, convinced that life is not worth living, about to jump to his death, your instinct would be to prevent him.

What, then, of a society '....which quietly encouraged the depressed, the inadequate, the isolated or the disabled to take their own lives; where doctors made available lethal mixtures for their patients; where suicides were left to get on with it. What kind of a society would that be? Would we wish to be members of it?' (Professor John Wyatt, '*Matters of Life and Death*', IVP, 1998, p.195).

Most civilised people would say 'No'. Your question mentions Holland, where voluntary euthanasia has been legalised. Already there is evidence there that non-voluntary euthanasia is now being performed, in situations where a life has been declared to be not worth living. This causes unease.

In a single short chapter, it is only possible to summarise some of the Christian challenges to euthanasia:

1. There is a difference between treatment decisions and value-of-life decisions. It is not for a doctor to pronounce whether someone's life is futile; only whether the treatment is futile. And even then, if the treatment is withdrawn, it should be because the treatment is valueless, *not because the patient is valueless.*

2. There is a difference between removing suffering and removing the sufferer. It is the difference between curing and killing. The hippocratic oath, enhanced by Christian teaching centuries later, was pledged to use treatment only; to help the sick – no more. 'I will not give poison to anyone, though asked to do so, neither will I suggest such a plan'. *The reason ought to be obvious; can the doctors be trusted?*

3. There is a difference between valuing someone for who they 'once' were, and valuing them for who they always are – and eternally will be. About the masterpiece of His creation, God has said, 'Whoever sheds the blood of man, by man shall his blood be shed; *for in the image of God has God made man'* (Genesis 9:6).

4. There is a difference between individual autonomy and shared community. As a community we are designed to depend upon each other, and for someone to opt out – *or be opted out* – is a blow struck at the identity of the whole family. It is no answer for the doctor to say, 'There is nothing more we can do for you'. The development of effective palliative care is the answer, and so is the development of the hospice movement, begun by Christians – a service that is virtually unknown in Holland.

Christians find suffering difficult – but it is built into our world-view. It has no purpose in the mind-set of unbelievers; hence their problem.

FOR FURTHER STUDY: John Wyatt, *Matters of Life and Death*, IVP, chapters 9-11.

66. Punishment for eternity?

I fail to see the justice of everlasting punishment for what may be only a few years or decades of sinful actions.

There are several ways of approaching this. First, on a purely human level, would we question the rightness of putting away someone who – in a couple of seconds of raging fury – had committed murder? I think not. The action might be over very quickly, but the repercussions would last for a long time.

Secondly, let us not minimise the nature of sin. Life is not a matter of balancing up good deeds against bad deeds – starting from a position of flat 'neutrality'. The human race as a whole is already in a state of rebellion. On the road of life, we are not faced with a fork ahead of us – and a choice between the good way and the bad way. The Bible teaches that we are, all of us, *already on the wrong road* (Romans 3:23). The picture is of us on a motorway, in desperate need of an exit road at the side, onto which we can transfer, and find safety.

The record of the Bible is that of God providing – at great and painful cost – the very escape route that we need. It is an exit clearly marked with signposts to help us leave our hellbound course. The 'signposts' include prophets, sacrificial foreshadowings, Bibles, churches, preachers, videos and Christian books. They are all pointing to the one way provided by the Cross. **If people are to miss the way of salvation provided by the death of Jesus, they will have to go past all that!** God has done everything necessary to bring us to Himself, and to safety.

We are shallow in our thinking about sin if we equate it only with a number of individual sinful acts. Our real situation as fallen beings is that every moment we live and breathe, we are in a state of rebellion against God. We are an offence to Him, unfit to spend eternity in His presence – unless something is done to deal with our offence and bring us safely to salvation.

The wonderful good news is that this has happened. God has opened up an escape route through the saving death of Christ – and we need no longer be an offence to Him – for Christ has borne that offence in His own suffering love, as a substitute in our place (2 Corinthians 5:21; Galatians 3:13). It is a free gift of His love.

Naturally, this is not automatic. *God inhabits Eternity. Do we want to spend it with Him?* It would obviously be quite illogical for someone to expect to have everything to do with Christ in the next life, when they have completely ignored Him in this.

Ultimately that is *the* sin that will inevitably take a person to destruction. If we by-pass the signposts, and finally ignore Christ's dying love for us, then we shall miss the one way of safety that He has provided in Himself.

67. Safer without the missionaries?

If it is the deliberate rejection of Christ that brings judgment, would not an individual or society have been safer without the missionaries?

Two corrections: we are all under judgment already; and secondly, no one is beyond the reach of Christ's voice (see chapter 37). That is the apostle Paul's argument: 'Did they not hear? Of course they did' (Romans 10:18). The problem is that, one way or another, we *have* heard the voice of the cosmic and eternal Christ, and in refusing the light, we are in darkness.

In your question you are logically saying, 'I myself would have been in a *safer* position if the good news of Jesus had been kept from me....It would have been safer if Britain could have been left under the spiritual leadership of the Druids....people in Europe, Africa or Asia were only exposed to greater peril when the early missionaries risked their lives to bring the Christian message to them....*It would actually have been safer if Christ Himself had not come at all.*'

Let's see where the flaws are, in this argument:

The Gospel does not create judgment – it lifts it. *It deals with the judgment that the whole human race already lies under.* Without God's saving action – the death of Christ for our sins – we are all without hope (Ephesians 2:12). The one and only way of removing our judgment was through the coming of the Gospel, and the preaching of its messengers.

Then we must realise that **those who are without the Gospel are not in a state of innocent neutrality.** Not at all. They are without hope. We sometimes hear the facile argument that it was a pity to disturb the primitive traditions and cultures of entire societies by bringing to them the 'alien'

Christian message. The assumption is that these societies were happy and contented in a paradise of their own. *But it never was paradise.*

Missionaries have often been criticised for going into Africa along the route carved out by the railways and commercial agencies of the British empire. But in point of fact it was the missionaries who held the key to the eventual freeing of the Africans from the all-dominating colonial interests. This was argued by the BBC documentary historian Jeremy Murray-Brown:

> Their message implied freedom from the ignorance of past centuries; freedom from the thraldom of malign spirits; freedom from the barriers to human progress imposed by tribal custom; freedom from the restraint on social and economic life requited by untamed natural forces. **Such a liberation of men's spirits must finally lead to a demand for personal and political freedom. The missionary gospel carried within it the seeds of decay to the imperial order itself.** *(Kenyatta,* George Allen and Unwin Ltd, 1972, p.41)

The implication of all this is that you and I ought to take up our missionary responsibilities to others immediately. There is no time to lose. If there had been any other way, outside of the Gospel, by which humanity could have been made 'safe', Jesus would never have come to die for us.

68. What makes a church a sect?

Any church is surely prone to error. But at what point does false teaching turn a church into a sect?

An identikit of a sectarian teacher is likely to show up in one or all of these five tendencies:

1. The truth-warpers. Gross and blatant error can usually be recognised instantly by most Christians. However, sectarianism advances by means of the part-truth – floated on apparently 95 per cent orthodoxy. A basic and biblically-credal topic, such as the eternal Sonship of Jesus Christ, or the resurrection of the body, will be taken and given a twist in a new direction.

2. The sheep-stealers. Because the sectarians have no true spiritual power residing in their distorted beliefs, they have to ride on the backs of those churches and evangelists that know and preach the truth. The sects cannot really evangelise. All they can do is *proselytise*; hovering on the edges of Christian fellowships and student groups, and using them as convenient sources of contacts. The membership of many sectarian groups often consists of untaught Christians.

3. The side-trackers. *Novelty* is the attraction. 'Those boring, dead sermons and Bible studies....here's something fresh that you never knew was in the Bible!' The way of the side-trackers is, first, to *dazzle*; secondly to *distort*; thirdly to *deceive* and fourthly to *divert*. Often it is the side-issues, the 'curiosities' of Scripture that move into the central area of their teaching. The final result is that unwary believers are seduced into leaving the mainstream of Christian living, and become locked in a side-water.

4. The peace-breakers. Sectarian groups will never see themselves as *part* of a wider fellowship. They will never be found in inter-church get-togethers, or take part in shared outreach programmes. They are IT! Consequently, if they ever gain a foothold in, for example, a Christian student group, they will never be content to follow the existing leadership. Rather, the tendency will be to undermine the leaders and infiltrate the membership, with a view to taking it over. If they get into a church, it won't be long before divisions are set up, and unity breaks down.

5. The power-brokers. The sects tend to rely upon a central, powerful and charismatic leading figure – or an all-dominating leadership circle, usually accountable to no one but themselves. All the arrows of attention are pointing *inwards* towards the leadership. Total loyalty is insisted upon. If the structure is that of a church, then the money and even the homes of its members, as well as their decisions and relationships, will be controlled by the leadership.

Such groups existed in New Testament days – against which the apostles warned their readers (Colossians 2:8; 2 Timothy 3:6,7). Who do we suppose were 'the Nicolaitans' (Revelation 2: 6,15)? Or who was being described in Jude 8–19 or 2 Peter 2: 12–18? These characteristics are all too evident in what at heart are only human-based organisations.

Christians who have become virtually owned by a sectarian-like group need to be reminded, 'Actually you are a disciple of one Man only.'

69. How do we recognise the occult?

I have heard about the Sixth and Seventh Books of Moses. Why are these books not part of the Bible?

True, there is a book that goes under that title – but Moses had nothing to do with it. The so-called Sixth and Seventh Books of Moses are *an occult work* – so named presumably because of the extra prestige derived from the name. The last time a copy came my way was as a result of an individual in a desperate extremity – handing the book over, in order to be rid of the evil influences that were destroying him. I burnt the book. The Devil's protection is promised to the person who owns it – and who wants that kind of protection?

Christ's coming has robbed the Devil of his power (Hebrews 2:14,15). It is by the **Name** of Christ, the **blood** of Christ, the **Word** of Christ, and by **prayer** in His authority that victory is assured over the world of occult (or '*hidden*') things. Yet although the Devil must give way to the power of Christ's death (Colossians 2:15), he is still an enemy, active and angry, knowing that his final end is approaching (Revelation 12:12).

Occultism has four main categories. First, *Superstition,* the venerating of little taboos – the idea being that an inanimate object can be invested with a force, or even personality. Secondly, there is *Fortune-telling,* in about thirty different forms, including use of pendulum, rods, astrology, card-reading and horoscopes. Thirdly, there is *Magic,* in some fifteen different forms, including both black and the supposedly 'white' (healing) magic. Fourthly, there is *Spiritism* – or its religious counterpart *Spiritualism* – in some thirty different guises, including table-lifting, levitation, glass-moving, ouija boards, speaking in trance, automatic writing, and clairvoyance.

Although fraud is sometimes part of the deal, these practices are to be firmly avoided – whether at the lesser level of the school playground experiment, or at that of deeper, deliberate involvement.

The Bible is completely hostile to all occult practice (see chapter 16). The reason is that 'the secret [Latin: *'occult'*] things belong to the Lord our God, but the things revealed belong to us and to our children....' (Deuteronomy 29:29). We are to explore all that God *has* revealed to us in His Word, but not the world of the departed and the unseen; they are in God's domain alone.

When Jesus is proclaimed in places where occultism has held sway, a reaction takes place. The dark powers have to retreat (Acts 19:18,19). Those taken over by evil spirits can be freed through Christ's authority, though only the experienced should undertake this ministry. Christians are safe from these powers – provided they do not transgress the boundaries.

There is a great difference, then, between magic and prayer. In magic, it is *humans* who are in the driving seat, trying to bend unseen powers to obtain a desired result. In prayer it is *God* who is handed the control; our part is prayerfully to place the entire issue before the heavenly Father, leaving the result to *Him*.

70. Fulfilment in the workplace?

I work with computers much of the day, and at times I feel like a machine myself. How, as a Christian, can I find encouragement in my work?

The apostle Paul would encourage you. 'Whatever you do', he declared to the slaves at Colosse, 'work at it with all your heart, as working for the Lord, not for men' (Colossians 3:23).

A slave in the Roman Empire was no more than an *instrumentrum vocale* – 'a tool that can speak'. Yet, for the most part, it was the slaves of Rome that provided the raw material for the Gospel to work on. What could provide them with a rationale of work?

1. Work needs a foundation – we find it in Creation

The first 'worker' was God Himself. He satisfied Himself that each stage of Creation was 'good'. The world was a garden, and humans – the summit of God's handiwork – were put into the garden to look after it.

This is basic. We are custodians, stewards of the Lord, and ultimately it is Him that we work for. The Creator gives to work its dignity and its normality.

2. Work needs rehabilitation – we find it in Christ

'It is the Lord Christ you are serving' (Colossians 3:24). Our human fall is what has adversely affected the workplace. Its relationships became soured, its environment became spoilt (Genesis 3: 17,18). Later, the prophets had to speak out against oppressive employers.

The rehabilitation process found its peak in Christ – Himself a working man. With the rise of Christianity, 'knowledge' (a favourite theme among the earlier Greek rationalists) became harnessed to energy and creativity. As

Faber's hymn later expressed it:

> A servant with this clause makes drudgery divine,
> Who sweeps a room, as for thy laws, makes that and the
> action fine.

The New Testament made redundant any thought of a special League Table of work. Financiers, panelbeaters and computer analysts – no category is higher than another. Fellowship around *Christ* and His Word provides a wonderful support to people in the workplace. Can you avail yourself of this? An early breakfast Bible study with friends, say once a week? Just to *remind* each other – our work, our speech, our relationships are to count for the Lord at the workplace!

3. Work needs a model – we see it in the slaves of the Roman empire

Slavery was an evil – but there in the Word of God lay the time bomb, quietly ticking away in the heart of the empire. Already Christians were learning to ignore the slave-master demarcation among themselves (Philemon 15 and 16). One day the entire movement would stand over the grave of the Caesars.

But in the meantime Christian slaves were called upon to give satisfaction (Titus 2:9). *They* were to be the setting for the bright jewel of the Christian Gospel. Life for them didn't begin when it was time to knock off work. Life was, and is, rising to each new day as a day of adventure with the Lord Jesus Christ – on Planet Earth.

71. Should Christians use force?

How can people of peace, like Christians, contemplate the use of force?

The violence of the opening years of the twenty-first century has taken our breath away. Terrorist activity and military conflict, and the resulting loss of life, can never, ever, be things of which the human race should be proud. The fact that these things cause us distress is not unhealthy – for they can drive us to prayer. Here now are some clarifying questions:

1. Do we believe in the validity of punishment?
The answer, surely, is Yes – if there is such a thing as objective truth and a given morality by which human life is ordered. If this were not so, we would have to remove from our vocabulary such words as 'reward', 'merit', 'justice' and even 'forgiveness'.

Punishment is not a popular word in circles that dislike the language of retribution, and speak rather of 'corrective treatment'. However, the apostle Paul is not afraid to speak of the secular authority as 'an avenger who carries out God's wrath on the wrongdoer' (Romans 13:4 ESV). The treatment of wrongdoing must have a retributive element in it, if it is ever to be corrective.

2. Is there a difference between force and violence?
The use of force is the disciplinary exercise of lawful authority – as seen, for example, in the powers of a democratically elected government, a well-regulated police force or a carefully controlled army. This is a valid part of God's order. Again, the apostle Paul puts it, 'Let every person be subject to the governing authorities....Whoever resists the authorities resists what God has appointed' (Romans 13:1,2 ESV).

It seems that 'force' becomes 'violence' when any of these authorities (and others too) become repressive. A situation can arise, when the ruling authority itself turns to violence. Revelation 13:5–8 portrays all such authorities as a repressive and blasphemous 'beast'. Then the call can indeed be for civil disobedience. The same principle applies when employers have become repressive, and strike action is legitimately called for. The earliest Trades Unions themselves were begun through Christian influence.

3. Do we assent to the depravity of the human heart?

This is the teaching that our historic fall into rebellion against God shows up in every area of our life (Jeremiah 17:9); that we cannot be trusted, and that societies and nations need agreed rules for our order and survival – rules that must be taken seriously. Without such restraints, and the appropriate power to apply them, chaos and anarchy are the result, as was evidenced biblically in the leaderless era of the Judges (Judges 21:25).

The believer should shun all forms of violence, but should be committed to the disciplined use of force. A great deal of muddled thinking takes place – especially during times of international conflict – when the debate fails to take account of the difference between violence and force. Force is concerned with the upholding of law. Violence is concerned with the overthrow of law.

72. The leading of the Spirit?

**I hear a lot of talk about people being 'led by the Spirit'.
How, in practical terms, does this happen?**

The classic passage is Romans 8. Verses 5–17 show that, in
fact, the actions of all three Persons of the divine Trinity are
involved in the enabling and 'controlling' of the Christian's
life (see especially vv. 9–11). To have the Spirit indwelling us
is evidently the same as having Christ indwelling us. And as
verse 6 puts it, 'The mind controlled by the Spirit is life and
peace' – this points to what John Stott calls *an inner
integration*.

When this happens to us, far from thinking or acting in a
series of uncoordinated or jerky decisions, we will be thinking
and deciding in a godly way, choosing and making judgments
in a manner that 'pleases God' (v.8). In the old Anglican
Prayer Book the only petition in the appointed prayer for
Whit Sunday is for *a right judgment in all things*. That may
not sound as exciting as being led by the Spirit to the right
parking spot in a city centre – but it is far more important.
To get it consistently *right* every time, in the numerous
decisions of our complicated living – there is no greater quality
that we could look for in a Christian worker or leader!

You ask how this happens. We are not to be like passive
animals which rely on bit and bridle for their guidance (Psalm
32:8,9). Nor have God's purposes anything to do with the
'fatalism' of some eastern belief-systems (see chapter 39). Being
'led' as a Christian is not an endless, hot-line seminar with
the Holy Spirit; nor are the minute details of the believer's
wardrobe, daily menu or holiday plans to be treated as issues
that require minute-by-minute guidance from the Holy Spirit.

The maturing believer is not to be like a child, who has to
be told at every turn, 'Brush your teeth, put your shoes on,
drink your milk!' Spirit-directed Christian living is never
infantile (1 Corinthians 14:20).

Further, the outlook that should characterise true mature decision-making will always be at odds with that of the Sectarian extremists. Such groups love to possess and control their members, and treat them as having no will of their own. They will require that all finances, even decisions about marriage, should be entrusted to their own authoritarian rule.

Confronted by many modern psychic epidemics, we learn to recognise that there is a thin dividing line in church life between the 'prophetic' and the 'hysteric' elements. **The place where we transgress the line and become unbalanced is at the point where the Scriptures – of which the Holy Spirit is Author – take second place to the areas of the Sensational and of 'feeling'.**

Jesus promised that His apostles, exclusively, would be led into all truth (John 16:13). *The New Testament was the fulfilment of this promise.* It is as our mindset is shaped by these Scriptures that we can begin to think as the *Spirit* would think – and therefore be led by Him.

73. Marriage – a submission?

I find words like 'submission' and 'obey' very unattractive, in the context of Christian marriage. Surely we've moved on from that?

It depends if we are culturally conditioned, rather than biblically taught! A key passage is Ephesians 5:21–33. In verse 31 the apostle Paul goes back to the creation principle that lies behind marriage – as Jesus did.

> For this reason a man will leave his father and mother and be united to his wife, and the two will become one flesh (Genesis 2:24).

Your 'unattractive' comment in reality derives from the damage done to marriage as a result of our human fall. Genesis 3:16 sums it up: 'To the woman [the Lord God] said... "Your desire will be for your husband, and he will rule over you."'

Here, *desire* is not to be seen as an attractive quality. It is the same word as that used in Genesis 4:7 where sin 'desires' to master Cain, in his murder of Abel. An ugly pattern in marriage, resulting from the Fall, is that of **conflict** – the wife with 'desires' of mastery over her husband, and the husband pursuing 'rule' over his wife. The loving, mutually submissive relationship thus degenerates into one of attempted mutual domination. That's where marriage tends to go if we leave it outside the redeeming power of God's good news in Christ.

This, says the New Testament, can be reversed. Wives are to *submit* to their husbands 'as to the Lord' (Ephesians 5:22), and husbands are to *love* their wives 'just as Christ loved the church' (v.25). Here is a mutual putting of the other first. 'Submit to one another out of reverence for Christ' (v.21). It means:

Wives submitting and not mastering
Husbands loving and not ruling

In both cases this is patterned after *Christ and the relationship he has with his church.* The wife submits to her husband, as head of the wife, as Christ is the head of the church. Christians do not have a problem with submitting to Christ as our Head – because as Saviour *he has loved us* enough to die for us. And husbands should not have a difficulty over doing everything for the benefit of their wives, if they are patterning themselves after Christ who died for the church. To die for their wives? Yes, if necessary – but at the very least giving themselves in everyday living. The designed result is a 'radiant' (v.27) wife...who radiates fulfilment.

It isn't just Paul. 'Wives', writes Peter, 'in the same way be submissive to your husbands' (1 Peter 3:1). *In the same way?* Peter is referring back to the example of **Christ's submission at the Cross**, 'entrusting himself to him who judges justly'. We can certainly say that there was **no weakness** in Christ's submission to his enemies, and **no inferiority**. And there was **no inequality**, in submitting his will to that of the Father. Christ's was a submission of great strength – and so, therefore, is the woman's in marriage at its best.

FOR FURTHER STUDY: Paul Williams on Ephesians 5:21–33 All Souls Audio Cassette Tape Library No. C113/05B (**vestry@allsouls.org**)

74. Does God allow divorce?

If a marriage ends in divorce – and perhaps a remarriage by one of the partners – how far does this take the person out of God's will?

Certainly when Jesus was asked about divorce (Matthew 19:2–9), the assumption would have been that a second marriage was implied. *Is this all right, 'for any and every reason?'* (v.3). There are tensions here that must be taken account of:

1. The tension between the ideal and the actual
The Pharisees would have had Deuteronomy 24:1–4 in mind, as they asked their question. But in Matthew 19:5, Jesus was far more concerned to quote the all-time ideal of *Marriage* in Genesis 2:24. That ideal is always to be our aim – while recognising that in the Gospel God does indeed meet people at their point of failure, and lead them on. We can live with this tension, once we understand it.

2. The tension between Law and Contingency
There were five different kinds of Law in the Old Testament – the *Creation* laws (relating to the Sabbath and marriage...), the *Covenant* laws (the Ten Commandments), the *Ceremonial* laws that would be fulfilled by Christ's sacrificial death, the *Compassion* laws of the prophets (that emphasised the internal motivation of the heart) – and the **Contingency laws.**

These were the 'What if?' laws, of Deuteronomy, chapters 12–25. Here, marriage is the ideal – *but is there a Plan B if something goes wrong?* Yes, there was. Read Deuteronomy 24:1–4, and notice the frequency of the word 'if' and 'and'. We are also given 'the exceptive clauses' of Jesus (*except for marital unfaithfulness* – Matthew 5:32; 19:9), as a divine, compassionate accommodation of human weakness. A similar clause is found in 1 Corinthians 7:12.

To the Pharisees, Deuteronomy 24 was a convenient **command** – for separation and divorce. To Jesus, it was a reluctant, yet gracious **concession**. For God ultimately wants to save, not separate – Christ's first priority being marriage, as the great ideal for the church to uphold. It still must be.

3. The tension between Discipline and Grace

Can God forgive, in the face of marital failure? The answer, through the Gospel of grace, is Yes. Otherwise where would King David have been after his sin of 2 Samuel 11? *No one need be written-off.* At the same time the church must, by its teaching and discipline, not allow marriage – the bedrock foundation of a stable society – to be eroded by lax practice. *No one else will attend to this priority.* This is why churches of every tradition need to have in place the disciplines that help everybody to protect Marriage and the Family; yet to do so with the very love of Jesus.

Celsus, the second century pagan critic, flatly disbelieved that the early Christians' upholding of marriage, was possible. 'There', commented the historian T.R. Glover, 'lay the great surprise.' The Christians, he wrote 'came with a message of the highest conceivable morality....they preached repentance and reformation, and people *did* respond; they repented and lived new lives'.

FOR FURTHER STUDY: John Stott, *New Issues Facing Christians Today,* IVP, chapter 14.

75. The rights of an unborn child?

At what point does an unborn child gain the right to live? How does this affect the issue of abortion?

Abortion – and with it, infanticide – was commonplace in the ancient world. Overpopulation, or the feared risk of 'a deformed child' would often be the motivation in Greek or Roman society. The general reasoning was that a child only acquired true identity at a period after birth, that its value lay only in its potential usefulness to society, and that only the likelihood of physical wholeness gave it a right to live. *Personhood had to be earned.*

This outlook was in marked contrast to the world of Judaism and the Old Testament law. The experience of the unborn child was highlighted, in retrospect, by the Psalmist:

> For you formed my inward parts; you knitted me together in my mother's womb. I praise you, for I am fearfully and wonderfully made. Wonderful are your works; my soul knows it very well. My frame was not hidden from you, when I was being made in secret, intricately woven in the depths of the earth. Your eyes saw my unformed substance; in your book were written, every one of them, the days that were formed for me, when as yet there were none of them (Psalm 139: 13–16 ESV).

This profoundly affects the very emotive issue of abortion: **At no point of an embryo's existence can the purely biological be separated from the spiritual.** The adult can later reflect, 'At no point was that little blob of protoplasm, anything other than ME.' *There is no moment, in the womb, of transition from animal to human.* This is common to all of humanity (Job 31:15. See also Jeremiah 1:5; Isaiah 49:5; Luke 1:41-44).

Thus the dualistic thinking that characterised early Greek society has to be confronted – for today it finds expression in the desire to create human embryos for the purpose of research, or providing spare parts. Also to be resisted is any thought of abortion *as a plan, programme or – as it has become in the West – an industry.*

When in 1967 the British Parliament reformed the abortion law, the not unworthy aim had been to clarify the law, to outlaw unprincipled abortions, and to give legality to doctors who terminated a pregnancy 'in exceptional cases'. The framer of the Bill, David Steel, declared, 'It is not the intention of the promoters of the Bill to leave a wide-open door for abortion on request.' *Yet this very thing happened.*

Today, concerned people are not powerless to take action. Organisations such as *CARE for the Family* (UK) and *Focus on the Family* (USA) deserve vigorous support, for their provision of education and pastoral care. Numerous pregnancy crisis centres exist today, offering counselling, short-term housing and support for those traumatised by the experience of an abortion.

The churches themselves have useful spokesmen. The paediatrics expert, Professor John Wyatt, writes in *Matters of Life and Death* (IVP), **'Nearly always, there is a better alternative to the unwanted or abnormal pregnancy than abortion'.**

76. Is sex restricted to marriage?

Hasn't the church been terribly repressed about sex? Is sexual expression really restricted to marriage?

Not in pagan circles of course. Demosthenes of old wrote, 'We keep prostitutes for pleasure; we keep mistresses for the day-to-day needs of the body; we keep wives for the begetting of children and for the faithful guardianship of our homes.' In Greek society sexual relationships between unmarried people were part of normal living. But as the Christian message collided with the Roman empire for the first time, it met the prevailing moral laxity head-on.

William Barclay has written, 'Chastity was the completely new virtue which Christianity brought into the world'.

The apostle Paul wrote, 'Avoid sexual immorality, that each of you should learn to control your own body in a way that is holy and honourable' (1 Thessalonians 4:3); *holy* in regard to our responsibility towards God, and *honourable* in our responsibility towards our neighbours. Paul goes on '...not in passionate lust like the heathen who do not know God'. There is implied here a vital relationship between the ignorance of God and moral laxity (see also Romans 1:18ff).

In Thessalonica, as in all Europe, the age-old assumptions of morality were about to be challenged, then undermined and finally replaced with a new ethic.
Every generation of Christians has to face this challenge – and it was harder by far for those believers of the first century. *Did we ever expect it would be easy?* We are following the purest Teacher in all of history; it is not surprising that the way is hard, revolutionary and against all the trends of society *in every age*. Genesis 2:24, as endorsed by Jesus and Paul, gives to us God's norm for the direction that is to be given to the sexual impulse. It amounts to fidelity in marriage, and celibacy outside marriage. That is what our Creator has given, as the

right, the safest way to channel the human sexual instinct.

The unbelieving world can't take it in. Tertullian of Carthage, in the second century, wrote of the Christians, 'So far from compromising in matters of sex, they are forbidden even a lustful look.' Several false assumptions about sex need to be challenged. Try and work on these:

1. Chastity is not truncation. Too often it is assumed that to have refrained from intimate relationships outside marriage means that you are only half a person. Not so; singleness – as long as it continues to be a Christian's situation – is a charismatic gift, a *charisma* (1 Corinthians 7:7).

2. Innocence is not ignorance. It is not the pursuers of purity who don't know about life – it is the promiscuous who don't even know what life is *for*.

3. Permissiveness is not freedom. It is as the permissive society has continued, that it has become greyer, more monotonous, and less able to deliver.

To speak of the church as needing to 'adapt' to the standards of its time would have been unacceptable to the writers of the New Testament. They expected things to change!

77. Same sex inclinations?

I am a Christian, and am beginning to wonder whether I am of homosexual orientation. Is there perhaps a church group of people similar to myself that I ought to join?

I wonder if we can defuse this issue a little? First, let's take out the word 'orientation'. It needs challenging. People talk as though there are only two basic kinds of human being – heterosexuals and homosexuals.

1. There are two categories only of human beings – male and female

The authors of the influential *St Andrew's Day Statement* (ceec@cableinet.co.uk) write that 'At the deepest ontological level....there is no such thing as 'a' homosexual or 'a' heterosexual; there are human beings, male and female....' This demarcation goes back to the very beginning of things (Genesis 1:27), and we should hold to it. Don't 'label' yourself *a homosexual* – however great the pressure from society.

Certainly we can speak of homosexual 'desires' and 'inclinations' – but the theory of a homosexual 'gene' that causes such desires has been well exploded. *If homosexuality was inherited*, a pair of identical twins would exhibit the same sexual characteristics – but there are plenty of documented cases where one twin will go in a homosexual direction, the other not. No, homosexual attractions are generally more likely due to 'an arrested juvenile state' (R.J. Berry, London professor of Genetics). Given time and space, an adolescent will make the transition to a more balanced outlook. *A great many obviously do.*

2. There are two callings only of sexual expression – marriage and singleness

Basic to our understanding of human sexuality are the first two chapters of Genesis. For Genesis 2:24 – endorsed by

Jesus and also by the apostle Paul – lays down the all-time divine ideal of a one man/one woman monogamous lifetime marriage. Christians should hold to this, rejecting *all* extra-marital sexual relationships (including homosexual activity).

We will find it a relief, if we can hold to this standard, for it will spare us endless speculation of the 'should we/shouldn't we?' variety. Pray about the person of the opposite sex that you may perhaps marry one day – if marriage is indeed to be your calling.

3. There are two responses of the Church – prophetic and pastoral

On the prophetic side it is up to the church to teach and preach on sexuality; and, while we have not always done this effectively, I note that the Anglican World 'Lambeth Conference' of 1998 voted massively against legitimising same-sex unions and the ordaining as clergy anyone involved in same-gender unions.

But, while 'rejecting homosexual practice as incompatible with Scripture', the conference also called for a sensitive and pastoral ministry to people of every sexual disposition.

No, I don't think the call is for you to join a group of others who are aware of homosexual feelings – but rather to be in a group simply of Bible-loving Christian people. Your protection, growth and strength for the future will stem out of ordinary, everyday New Testament fellowship.

FOR FURTHER STUDY: John Stott, *Same Sex Partnerships?* All Souls Audio-tape Library, No. H1/25 (vestry@allsouls.org)

78. Special prayer for healing?

What is the right place of prayer for healing in public evangelistic meetings? Should we encourage our church members to attend?

In praying for the sick, the best place of all is the local church fellowship. There we find the surest platform of all. It is there that we know each other; it is there that we can monitor the progress – and perhaps learn from our mistakes. Let's be biblical:

> Is any one of you suffering? Let him pray. Is anyone cheerful? Let him sing praise. Is anyone among you sick? Let him call for the elders of the church, and let them pray over him, anointing him with oil in the name of the Lord. And the prayer of faith will save the one who is sick, and the Lord will raise him up (James 5:13-15 ESV).

Note the language. *It is for the sick person* to call for the church leaders to come and pray; so no unwelcome pressure is brought to bear upon the sufferer. Then they are to pray 'over' him; the implication is that this is more than a trivial ailment; it is something that has prostrated the individual.

The oil? This may refer partly to the accepted medicine of New Testament days – implying that medicine and prayer belong together. We are never to despise medical means. But oil is also symbolic of the Holy Spirit. And anointing was a biblical way of clearly identifying before the Lord who was the particular focus of the prayers at that moment.

The prayer of faith will **save** *the one who is sick.* Yes, the Greek word is ambiguous. It can certainly mean that the ill person will be restored physically. But it can equally refer to spiritual blessings resulting from prayer. Indeed, it can even imply – in the event of ensuing death – a resurrection confidence for the next life. *Whatever the outcome,* 'the Lord will raise him up'. Many times, as a church pastor, I have said to someone, after prayer of this kind, 'The Lord will raise you up. It says so!'

It should be made known in the local church that prayer of this kind is available. Learn from Jesus. When he healed, it was always personal; I don't seem to read of mass healings in the Gospels. And Jesus needed no platform, no special lights or music, and no single routine or formula.

It is partly for these several reasons that I tend to be wary of big rallies that give advance publicity of healings and miracles as part of the programme. Further, the credentials of the healing practitioners at the front need to be investigated. **What do they believe? What to them is the Gospel? Were they ever involved in clairvoyance or mediumism? How is money handled in their organisation? What about the follow-up and the monitoring of the results?**

Can God heal directly today? Yes, He can. But if healing is given, it comes as a by-product of the Gospel. It is not the Gospel itself (see chapter 31).

79. I want to learn to pray

How can I learn to pray? I feel inadequate and ashamed. My thoughts wander, and I have no discipline. How can I get off the ground?

You're not alone in your desire. 'Teach us to pray', said Christ's disciples. No mature Christian that I've ever met has left the learners' lane when it comes to prayer. But let's not stay defeated on the ground, dolefully signalling for the ambulance. *Just begin.*

Get into the habit – **as you wake up** – of greeting the glorious Trinity! Another day of Adventure on Planet Earth – with the Lord Jesus Christ! Dedicate that day to God the Father – even while your head is still on the pillow. Even before you're out of bed, and as the film of the day in front of you begins to roll on the screen of your mind, ask that the Holy Spirit will fill you *now*, to be a servant of the Lord right through the day. Isn't that worth doing? And now what? A glass of water? A cup of tea? And then....?

Work it out. Obviously time with God is well spent early in the day (see chapter 55). But if there are children who have to be got up, or if work demands a very early start, then some other part of the day may be set aside. I don't think that a quiet time on the Metro, or on a bus is to be despised at all – why, I've seen a Muslim doing this with the Koran in London's Euston Station. So why not you?

Given this, there is a strong call for Christians to learn the practice of unhurried intercession – that is, praying on our knees on behalf of people, places, churches and world events (1 Timothy 2:1–8). When we do this, we are being 'priests' – acting for God on behalf of others. **We pray; He works.** Intercessory prayer is God's appointed means by which we may co-operate with the achieving of his will within his world.

Keep it short, to begin with, and believe that your capacity will grow. When prayer is happening, an unstoppable power is let loose. We have only to look at the example set by our praying friends where the church is sensationally growing.

Write a list of names and places. Keep it on your person. Have different names for each day. 'I pray for you on the nineteenth day of every month', Bishop Alf Stanway of Australia once told me. I was stunned.

But you can do that. **It is possible for intercessors to wield as much influence in countries that they have never been to, as if they were there themselves.** Adopt a country. Get the news about it. Keep newspaper clippings. List the names of those church leaders and mission representatives.

And let's set ourselves targets. 'I used to pray for fifty people a month to become followers of Jesus in my area,' a smiling African leader told me. 'Now I'm praying for a hundred a month!'

80. How to get a Church praying

Although our church is Bible-based, we don't actually have a church prayer meeting. Does this matter, in view of our Sunday services?

Well....do you want your church *really* to be Bible-based? If so, I think you will find the will and the means to get those occasions set up for specific, united prayer. Learn from the apostle Paul:

> First of all, then, I urge that supplications, prayers, intercessions and thanksgivings be made for all people, for kings and all who are in high positions, that we may lead a peaceful and quiet life, godly and dignified in every way. This is good, and it is pleasing in the sight of God our Saviour, who desires all people to be saved and to come to the knowledge of the truth (1 Timothy 2:1-4 ESV).

Here is clearly expressed the priority of prayer in the organising and leading of the church's life. Joint prayer – it's axiomatic in the work of the church. As a matter of fact, it *is* the work. Some observations:

1. The praying church is a school of prayer
Prayer in the church is an education. Notice the variety – *supplication, prayers, intercessions, thanksgivings.* 'Heaven fights for those who pray', said a Christian preacher. United prayer protects the fellowship, stretches faith, enriches experience and widens our view – both upwards to the Lord, and sideways to the farthest horizons.

2. The praying church is a corner-shop of prayer
Do you have an Asian corner-shop in your area? We do, and there – unlike the out-of-town mega store – we witness intimacy, service and the potential to build a community of trust. Even more should this be true with the gathering for

prayer of Christians who know each other – the result in the community can be what Paul calls 'a peaceful and quiet life'.

The prayer meeting, then, should be central to the life of the church's programme. It should be held on a night when nothing else is organised. No one should be elected to eldership in the church unless they understand that they are expected to be at the prayer meeting. No leader or worker should be appointed until they pledge that they will be there. **The leader or pastor, will forsake all outside speaking engagements on prayer meeting night, personally leading it, and blocking the date off right through the year.**

3. The praying church is a web-site of prayer

The slogan ought to be, *Our church could touch the world.* Have you noticed the universal scope of prayer in the passage? *For all people....kings....all those in high positions....desire all people to be saved.*

No church should aim to be a mega church. But every fellowship should aspire to be **a world church** – with threads of influence and power leading out from it....everywhere. 'It is prayer, and prayer alone', wrote Jacques Ellul, 'that can make history'.

Part Five

The Christ we follow

When a portrait is spoiled, the only way to renew it is for the subject to come back to the studio and sit for the artist all over again. That is why Christ came – to make it possible for the divine image in man to be re-created.

We were made in God's likeness; we are re-made in the likeness of his Son.

(Athanasius of Alexandria, AD296-373: translation from *After the Gospels,* David Winter, Mowbrays, London)

81. Jesus – The only one to follow?

How can I be confident that Jesus is the ultimate figure, in all history, for us to follow?

The human race is haunted by Jesus Christ. Films, books and articles proliferate. Often they present a very distorted view. But it is about *him*, rather than other religious leaders that the debate continues. And 'deities' that were huge in their time have all in turn been obliterated by this one great Name.

Even figures of history only fleetingly associated with Christ have become universally famous. We would never have heard of Pontius Pilate – but for the single meeting with Jesus that made Pilate's the second best-known name in all history; *'He was crucified under Pontius Pilate'* is declared worldwide in churches every Sunday.

Children everywhere have been named after Christ's disciples. 'In years to come,' wrote Andrew Knowles, 'people would call their dogs "Caesar", and their sons "Matthew"; just one of the changes Jesus makes!' (*The Way Out*, Collins). But take it further still. Here are some pointers:

1. Christ's unique character
Few will say that Jesus was anything other than supremely good (see chapter 61). His goodness was endorsed by *his friends* (1 Peter 2:22) who had every opportunity to see him at close range; also by *his enemies* who could not make a single charge against him stick. Most remarkably of all, *he himself* made the claim of sinlessness (John 8:46). This was unlike all spiritual leaders, before or since, who, the more they advanced in character, became increasingly aware of their own moral imperfection.

2. Christ's unprecedented conduct
Let me list only a few. *Christ forgave people their sins* – even the sins that they had committed against individuals whom

Jesus had never met. This provoked the charge of blasphemy, for 'Who can forgive sins but God alone?' (Mark 2:5-7). Further, *Jesus accepted the worship of people* (John 20:28). True, there are 'gurus' today who receive worship, but they invariably end up in a tomb. *Jesus rose from the dead.*

3. Christ's unparalleled claims

Jesus made numerous claims, including that he was *the Son of God* in a unique sense (John 1:18). His relationship to 'the Father' was such that he would refer to 'my Father and your Father' (John 20:17); never to 'our Father' – except in the case of the Lord's Prayer when it was his followers who should so pray. And Jesus did not hesitate to use the divine name 'I am' of himself (John 8:58).

Further, Jesus claimed to be *Universal Judge* (Matthew 7: 22, 23; John 5: 22, 23). No one else ever claimed the right to decide upon the eternal destiny of all people. Lastly, Christ claimed to be *the Centre of all truth,* drawing all types and conditions of humanity to himself (John 12:32, 46; 14:6).

Either Jesus was what he claimed to be, or he was not. No claimant who was *wrong* – on such massive issues – could possibly be 'mistaken'; he would have to be mad. But madness has never been attributed to Jesus.

FOR FURTHER STUDY: Chris Wright, *Thinking Clearly about the Uniqueness of Jesus*, Monarch Publications

82. Who is the real Christ?

Books, plays, paintings and even preachers have got me somewhat confused as to what Jesus is really like. What is he on about? What is his game plan?

This question was asked by an enquirer in the *Christianity Explored* course at All Souls Church in London. Certainly a whole galaxy of 'Christ' figures tends to be paraded by groups and organisations anxious to attract people to their programmes, to suit *their* own 'game plan'.

People have been doing this ever since Christ's first hearers tried to turn him into a liberator from the Roman occupation. Even Herod, at the time of Jesus' trial, hoped that the prisoner might turn Entertainer (Luke 23:6–8).

And so, across the centuries, we have been waylaid by the *Military Christ* of the ill-conceived Crusades, but, in contrast, by the *Sentimental Christ* of English Victorian gentility. The Christ who has been called upon to bless battleships in one generation can be invoked to bless guerrilla fighters in the next. In our own time we have been faced by the claims of Jesus the *Political Messiah*; alternatively by those of a *Social Programme Christ*. Showbusiness people have interpreted Jesus as a *Superstar Christ*; religious existentialists as a *Signs and Wonders* miracle worker.

Through the ages there has been an *Artists' Christ*; he has been painted youthful and virile, pale and emaciated, severe and majestic, ethereal and remote. There is a *feminine* version of Christ, or the Ché Guevara-like image of *the revolutionary*. Jesus has, in turn, been *a clown, a dancer, a radical, a tramp*. It is the way of what is called Postmodernism, to encourage the creation of your own *Designer Christ*, who can be cut and pasted to fit your particular programme.

Perhaps it is around the word *programme* that we can establish an answer to the question. On the whole, those who wish to adopt a Christ of their own making have defined him by what he can 'do' for their chosen cause. But is *our* 'game plan' *his?*

Who is he? What did he come for? When we consult the primary documents that tell us of Jesus Christ, we are forced to conclude that he has his own programme – preset and ordained from eternity, for he is **'the Lamb that was slain from the creation of the world'** (Revelation 13:8). The answer lies precisely there (see also chapter 27).

The *programme* for his representatives and agents, then, is made very clear by the apostle Paul:

> I decided to know nothing among you except Jesus Christ
> and him crucified   (1 Corinthians 2:2).

The validity of the Christ that you call upon stands or falls by the test of the Cross. In Jesus' own words, 'The Son of Man came not to be served, but to serve, and to give his life as a ransom for many' (Mark 10:45). If your 'Christ' did not come to die for the sins of the world, and to bear their penalty, you had better change your Christ at once.

FOR FURTHER STUDY: *Christianity Explored* – an enquirers' course: **www.christianityexplored.com**

83. The truth – in one man?

I struggle to understand how in one man, Jesus, we can know God, and the truth about all of life. Can you help?

Read John's Gospel. Just to read it has helped millions. By the time the reader arrives at chapter 5, the conviction is growing, *This Man is God. He knows everything.*

'Logic is the Logos', wrote Athanasius of the fourth century AD. He was referring to John 1:1–14, where Christ is identified as *The Word* (Greek: '*Logos*'). By 'Logic' Athanasius meant the methodology, the rationale, **the explanation** of something. If, for example, you understand 'the logos' of meteorology, or of biology, then you understand its nature, its purpose and direction.

As far as *life itself* is concerned, Jesus is both its goal and starting point (see chapters 1 and 24). Athanasius helped the church to understand this truth afresh during the controversies that boiled up around the nature of Christ's person. As he put it: **Only Jesus, as God, can reveal God.**

The *English Standard Version* of the Bible is helpful in its translation of John 1:18: 'No one has ever seen God; the only God, who is at the Father's side, he has made him known.' This 'Revealer' – who is the same as God – is, of course, Jesus. Matthew 11:27 gives us the same truth from the words of Christ himself.

In the face of false teachers, such as Arius – who maintained that Christ was 'similar to' God, but not 'the same as' God – Athanasius was adamant; his faithfulness to Scripture was rewarded at last in the Council of Nicea in AD325. Its statement has become part of the historic church creed. There it is said of Christ that he is ...*God of God, Light of Light, Very God of very God, Begotten, not made, Being of one substance* (the vital word) *with the Father....*

Some people ask, 'Can the **Son** of God be truly God?' Yes – this is our understanding of the Trinity (chapter 22). Christ is of the same *substance,* essence or nature as the Father. It was with all due reverence that the evangelist Vijay Menon once colourfully illustrated it, 'The son of a tiger is a tiger; the son of a baboon is a baboon; the Son of God...is *God'.*

There is unanimity in the New Testament on this truth. The term 'The Lord' (Greek: *kurios*) is used fourteen times of **God** in the opening chapter of Luke's Gospel. Then, in the rest of the Gospel the same word is used fourteen times of **Jesus Christ**. The implication is obvious; *Jesus is the Lord God.*

> He [Christ] is the radiance of the glory of God and the exact imprint of his nature (Hebrews 1:3 ESV).

In all the Letters of the New Testament, Christ is referred to only twenty-two times by his human name, Jesus; but 701 times by some form of expression that acknowledges his deity.

Jesus is fully God and fully man. 'It followed', wrote Athanasius, 'that he alone was able to recreate everything and to be an ambassador for all men with the Father.'

84. Jesus – why a virgin birth?

I can't see why the virgin birth of Jesus is important. Please explain.

The virgin birth of Jesus is taught in the Scriptures, and is affirmed in all the historic Christian creeds. *It has nothing to do with any supposed Christian belief that human sexual relationships were in themselves sinful and were therefore inappropriate to the birth of the Son of God.*

And forget all notions, common in pagan literature, of deities having sexual relations with humans. What the Bible account reverently presents is the combination of Christ's **manward** side (the human name – *Jesus* – and the human birth), and the **Godward** (*Son of God* – and the supernatural conception).

Both Gospels of Matthew and Luke, independently of each other, feature infancy stories of Jesus. Both are in clear agreement that the conception of the child was not caused by the involvement of an earthly father, but rather through the direct, supernatural intervention of the Holy Spirit. In Matthew 1:23, the Old Testament prophecy of Isaiah 7:14 is quoted, **'Behold, the virgin shall conceive and bear a son, and they shall call his name Immanuel'.** Virgin (*'parthenos'*) represents a word in the Hebrew text that means a 'young woman' – with the implication of course that this is a pure, unmarried woman.

Mark's Gospel has no cause to mention the virgin birth – for it begins not with the birth of Jesus, but with his public ministry. And the Gospel of John begins on a different level altogether, developing further the profound truth of the Incarnation.

It is really the virgin *conception* of Jesus that was miraculous; the *birth* was like that of any baby. The key passage for our understanding – for which the *English Standard Version* provides the best translation – runs as follows:

> And Mary said to the angel, 'How will this be, since I am a virgin?' And the angel answered her, 'The Holy Spirit will come upon you, and the power of the Most High will overshadow you; therefore the child to be born will be called holy – the Son of God' (Luke 1:34,35 ESV).

*Therefore....*The obvious conclusion to be drawn from the angel's words is that the birth of **a truly holy human being** was the chief outcome of this miraculous event. The virgin birth is not, in itself, a proof of Christ's deity; even Muslims believe in the virgin birth. Nor did Jesus *become* Son of God at his conception and birth; he is eternally Son. Rather, we have in this teaching the God-given indication that *the normal physiological process, by which our inherited fallen sinful human nature was passed on from generation to generation, was to be arrested.*

Consequently, Jesus – though God incarnate – grew and developed as a normal human being (Luke 2:40,50,51). Yet despite experiencing human temptations as we do, he was without sin (Hebrews 4:15; 7:26). He is then, the only human being who can credibly stand for us, speak for us – and suffer for our sins.

85. Did Jesus rise bodily?

Must we be held to the crudeness of a literal resurrection of Jesus Christ? Is it not enough to describe the Easter event as a wonderful metaphor of the Christian hope?

Certainly there are books written by supposed academics that solemnly put forward such theories. But we only need ten minutes' thought to realise that we are in dreamland if we think like that. *Just think!*

Here are twelve men whose world has come to an end. One of them is already dead – by his own hand. Another has himself publicly denied that he had ever met Jesus, and retires from the scene a broken man. Yet another takes the mother of the crucified leader, to look after her in his own home. It looks like an obvious end-of-story sequel. There is also a pessimist in the group – who had forecast disaster all along (John 11:16).

It only takes the confusion of a night arrest to cause the twelve to disintegrate completely (Matthew 26:56). What caused them ever to come together again – to the extent that their enemies would describe them as 'these men who have turned the world upside down' (Acts 17:6 ESV)? *A metaphor? Beautiful picture language?* Please! As well as the empty tomb, there are the changed disciples that have to be explained.

We hear from time to time of someone who has managed to come back from a death (or near-death) experience. Even to the extent of being nailed down in the coffin first! **But how long does the excitement last?** I can just remember such an event. A man had 'died', and then made the come-back. The news item just squeezed into the BBC *World at One* news programme. I never saw it featured in any paper. And the man's name? I'd forgotten it within ten minutes. Presumably it will be on a gravestone one day.

If Jesus Christ had not clearly – and unequivocally – been raised bodily as the permanent conqueror of death on behalf of the human race, we would never have heard of him. The demoralised movement would have fizzled out on the launching pad. For a while, memories of a carpenter-healer would have persisted around Galilee; then 'The Jesus Event' would have ended up like *The Theudas Event* (Acts 5:36), washed over like a child's sandcastle on the beach by the tides of history – until the three-year blip would be flattened out as though it had never been.

Look at 1 Corinthians 15:3-5, where, *in a single, unbroken sentence,* Christ is the subject of four verbs; He died, was buried, was raised, and appeared. Implication: **what was raised was what was buried.**

Do the metaphor theorists think Jesus actually died? *Yes, yes.* Was buried? *Sure.* Was raised on the third day? (Always that insistence on 'the third day'!) *Er, no – that's metaphorical.* Appeared? *No, that's metaphorical too.*

So within a single sentence, Paul can switch from factual language to metaphorical language? **Please!....**

FURTHER READING: Richard Bewes, *The Resurrection: Fact or Fiction?* Lion Publishing. See also chapter 50.

86. Evidence for the ascension?

I have been challenged by a critic that there is no evidence among the Gospel writers that Jesus ascended to heaven; that Mark 16:19 is not part of the original Greek text, and that Luke 24:51 is not supported by the best early manuscripts. How valid is this criticism?

You are referring to the phrase that Jesus 'was carried up into heaven'. Certainly Mark 16:9–20 comes within the category of a footnote rather than the main Gospel text (see chapter 48). But although not *all* the early Greek manuscripts of Luke 24:51 include the phrase *and was carried up into heaven*, '**it is found in manuscripts and versions of the highest character, and ought certainly to be retained**' (W.B. Jones DD, *The Speaker's Commentary,* 1878). Supporting documents include the major 'Alexandrinus' and 'Vaticanus' manuscripts (see chapter 41).

Actually, if your questioner had read more widely, he would have learnt that Christ's Ascension is a theme running through the Scriptures.

1. The Ascension of Jesus is consistent with the ancient prophecies
Psalm 68:18 which refers to 'God' ascending on high, and leading captives in his train, is quoted in the New Testament, and directly connected with the Ascension of Jesus (Ephesians 4:7–10). Other references include Psalms 47:5; 110:1.

2. The Ascension of Jesus is recognised as the goal of the Gospel story
Your friend evidently missed other instances of the phrase in question: 'As the time approached for him *to be taken up to heaven....*' (Luke 9:51). The Ascension is seen here as the end goal of Christ's journey, the triumphant celebration of his saving work at the Cross.

3. The Ascension of Jesus was directly announced by himself
The risen Jesus told Mary Magdalene, 'Do not cling to me,
for *I have not yet ascended* to the Father; but go to my brothers
and say to them, "*I am ascending* to my Father and your Father,
to my God and your God"' (John 20:17 ESV). It couldn't be
clearer.

**4. The Ascension of Jesus was directly reported by the
Gospel writers**
Luke 24:51 has already been referred to. But here is Luke again
in his sequel book, the Acts of the Apostles. He declares that
his Gospel took the reader through the story of Jesus '*until
the day when he was taken up....*' (Acts 1:2). Luke now goes on
to relate how '*....he was lifted up*, and a cloud took him out of
their sight' (Acts 1:9). Clear enough?

**5. The Ascension of Jesus is interpreted in the light of his
return**
Luke again – 'And while they were gazing into heaven as he
went, behold, two men stood by them in white robes and
said, "Men of Galilee, why do you stand looking into heaven?
This Jesus *who was taken up from you into heaven* will come in
the same way as you saw him go into heaven"' (Acts 1:10,11
ESV).

**Let's get these and other references into our heads (John
6:62; 16:28; Acts 3:21 ESV; Ephesians 1:20–22). We want to
help both ourselves and our friends about the ascended
triumph of our Lord.**

87. What is Jesus doing in heaven?

What is meant by the idea of Jesus praying or interceding for us in heaven? Why does he need to do that?

Some have mistakenly thought that our Lord is somehow 're-offering' the sacrifice of his death before the Father in heaven, and in so doing is 'pleading' on our behalf. It is even claimed in some circles that this happens during the service of Holy Communion – that in a special way the Cross of Calvary is being *freshly presented* in heaven at that moment, for the forgiveness of our sins.

But that would be to deny the 'once-for-all' nature of what took place when Jesus died for the sins of the world, at a certain time and place in history. At the Transfiguration, Moses and Elijah were seen, speaking with Jesus about the 'departure' (literally 'exodus') that Jesus would accomplish for the sins of the world when he died. We read that this was not to take place in heaven, *but on earth, at Jerusalem* (Luke 9:30,31). The New Testament is clear in its insistence that Christ's death was historically once and for all achieved, and never to be repeated, or re-offered:

> ....**He is able to save to the uttermost those who draw near to God through him, since he always lives to make intercession for them....He has no need, like those high priests, to offer sacrifices daily, first for his own sins, and then for those of the people, since he did this once for all when he offered up himself** (Hebrews 7: 25,27 ESV).

It is already done. Only when we have understood that a way into the Father's presence has been fully and finally secured, can we really take in the wonder of the atonement – and of Christ's present ministry on behalf of his followers. His work he came to do on earth is finished. What, then, is he doing now, in heaven?

The Christian is assured that, in virtue of Christ's unrepeatable, sacrificial death, he is now in heaven as Man (not an 'ex-man') **to represent us before the Father** (1 John 2:1). It is in *that* sense that he may be said to be 'pleading' for us.

No, this is not a continuous (or repeated) *re-offering* of the sacrifice of the Cross; that would be to undercut the certainty and finality of our redemption. Nor is Christ's 'intercession' a continuous stream of uttered petitions.

The thrilling truth is that Jesus Christ is ever-living in heaven, *to support our case, to guarantee our complete forgiveness, and to escort us into the Father's presence every time we turn to God's throne in prayer.* Any time I desire to approach the Father, Christ is there at the Father's side, as the One who died for me, to ensure that I get a hearing! There is a Man in heaven, a perfect Man; our Intercessor. That is why Christian prayer ends with 'In Jesus Christ's Name'. He is our *only* way through.

88. Jesus – and the Holy Spirit?

What was happening at Pentecost? Is this an extra dimension, on top of following Jesus and being born again?

Not exactly. Pentecost, rather, is the thrilling *fulfilment* of Christ's earlier promise of the New Birth and the Spirit's indwelling power – on an international scale. Luke's Gospel ends with Jesus pledging, 'I am going to send you what my Father has promised' (Luke 24:49). Luke's book of Acts was to be the exhilarating sequel.

Supposing the book of Acts had been lost? We would have found it almost impossible to explain the phenomenal power and boldness of the early Christians. For the book opens with the historic gathering of Pentecost; with the sound of the rushing mighty wind, the flames of fire that settled on the disciples, and the miracle with which the amazed listeners heard the Gospel being announced to them – each in their own language (Acts 2:1–13). Pentecost gave the Gospel of the New Birth an international platform! It was a *unique* event, a *universal* event and a *saving* event.

All this had been prophesied in the Old Testament – as Jesus explained when teaching Nicodemus about the New Birth (see chapter 28). He had taught his disciples that the Holy Spirit, 'another Counsellor', would come and indwell them (John 14:16–18). Not a *different* Counsellor, but, as the New Testament Greek implies, a *second* Counsellor or 'Helper' (ESV) who would be the 'other', unseen presence of Jesus himself, accessible to believers in China, the Americas or Africa....

We can illustrate. Picture a pop star coming down the aeroplane gangway at Seoul Airport. A thousand fans are eagerly waiting – just for a glimpse. Maybe four or five might even get an autograph? However, the contact can only be disappointingly limited. After a few minutes the celebrity steps into a car and is driven away. But later that evening comes the explanation. There on the screen, in the TV concert, is the same familiar person – now made accessible to millions of fans, by another medium.

Christ was taken away from the few, in order to become accessible to the many – to believers on every continent. Through 'another Counsellor' (the third Person of the Trinity), the very presence of Christ himself is brought into your one-room flat, but (*better* than a pop star) right into your heart and life.

When we have been born again, we sense that 'Christ has come into my life'. That is true. *Christ* has become real to us, as our Lord, and ever-present companion. However, technically speaking, it is the Holy Spirit who, as Christ's 'other self', has taken up residence.

It is because the Spirit magnifies *Christ* (John 16:14), that there is a certain anonymity about the Counsellor. A Spirit-filled person is, inevitably, a Christ-centred and Christ-aware person (see chapter 33). The Spirit is the Executive of the Godhead. **He comes to accomplish IN us all that Jesus came to do FOR us at the Cross** – making forgiveness and the Lord's friendship a personal reality, all our days.

89. How is Christ coming back?

Isn't the idea of Jesus of Nazareth returning to earth a bit quaint to accept, in our computerised world of e-mails and the Internet?

Not if we have studied the Bible. Many people today have an incredibly feeble conception of the future; it is vague and wishy-washy – and it follows that the present won't make much sense for them at all. *It is only when you can see where the world and history are heading, that the present – your own present – is lit up with meaning and purpose.*

The coming of the Lord Jesus Christ will take place personally, powerfully, bodily, visibly, publicly – and *instantly*. Read Matthew 24:30,31, or 1 Thessalonians 4:13-5:3. It will be quicker than any e-mail. Here are words of Jesus:

> For as the lightning flashes and lights up the sky from one side to the other, so will the Son of Man be in his day (Luke 17:24).

This will be no local happening ('Look there!' or 'Look here!' – Luke 17:23). That day, the world won't be seeing the Carpenter of Nazareth, wearing Galilean homespun. It will be Jesus in his incandescent brilliance as the 'Son of Man', as foreseen by Daniel, back in the Old Testament (Daniel 7:13,14). Centuries later, Peter, James and John were to witness their familiar Master 'transfigured', as the same irradiated Person – in a dramatic preview of Christ's triumphant final rule (Luke 9:28–36).

The martyred Stephen, about to die, had a similar glimpse: 'Behold I see the heavens opened, and the Son of Man standing at the right hand of God' (Acts 7:56). The exiled apostle John on the island of Patmos saw the same figure: '....*his face was like the sun shining in full strength'* (Revelation 1:16). The whole world will finally witness this same spectacle (Revelation 1:7). The return of Christ will mark the end of history, as we know it. It will inaugurate the final Judgment. It will re-unite the Lord with his church on earth. It will bring about the new heaven and the new earth. Pain, death, persecution, privation and sorrow will all be banished. The entire edifice of evil that has raised itself against the rule of God will be dismantled in a moment. As a modern hymn expresses it:

> One day great Babylon will tell its ashen story,
> Drunk with her worldly power, her sins piled to the sky;
> Standing astride her grave, the martyred saints in glory
> Sing their hallelujahs as the smoke goes up on high.
>   (R.T. Bewes, Jubilate Hymns: jubilateMW@aol.com)

We have been warned all along not to place a date or a time upon the Second Coming of Christ (Matthew 24:42-44). Many people ignore this warning and waste endless time in their calculations. The way in which we should be spending our days before the end, is to work, watch and witness – whether or not yours is a world of computers, e-mail and all the rest!

FOR FURTHER STUDY: Anne Graham Lotz, *The Vision of His Glory* (Word Publishing); Richard Bewes, *The Lamb Wins* (Christian Focus).

90. A synthesis of traditions?

Is there anything against holding multi-religious services? After all, would it not be helpful to combine the best of all the world's beliefs?

Always our attitude towards those of other belief-systems must be one of firmness, combined with courtesy and grace. We do well to be aquainted with those of other beliefs, and at times to engage in discussion and open debate. Indeed it is not impossible for Christian believers to attend an event organised by people of another religion – provided it was understood that we were present in an attitude, not of participation, but of respectful 'observance'.

But we still have to remember that those who reject Christ's claims are outside his covenant, and are lost people – and desperately need the good news of his saving death for the sins of the world. *And no one is beyond the reach of his voice* (see chapter 37).

Once let it be implied that faith in Christ is but one of many possible alternatives, and we have thrown over the very principle for which the first-century Christians were thrown into the arena, or burnt to death. In those days of the Roman Empire, they were killed, not because they believed that Jesus was divine – for the political authorities allowed for as many gods as you liked.

They were killed because they insisted that Jesus was the only Lord. He was to be worshipped and followed exclusively, as against every contending saviour, messiah, or Caesar-god. They refused to accept a place for Christ, in a 'coalition' alongside other 'gods' in the Roman *Pantheon*. By teaming up with another religion, you are saying, 'As a Christian, I am wrong'.

The prophet Elijah had to combat a similar mindset, when confronted by the prophets of Baal (1 Kings 18). People must have argued with Elijah, 'These Baal–worshippers are really pretty decent people, you know. They aren't all that different from us. It would be an *enrichment* to do a deal with them.' But Elijah wouldn't have it – and the result was the preservation of God's unique revelation.

Throughout, the Bible presents a single, integrated unity of thought, in the only true God *who is defined as the God and Father of our Lord Jesus Christ* (see chapters 1 and 24). It is meaningless to talk in vague terms of 'God'....something/ Someone out there – as though that title can incorporate every contrasting and contradictory belief in sight. In discussion, the courteous challenge we should put to representatives of other religions is, 'Please describe your relationship to the Jesus Christ of space, time and history.'

A synthesis of beliefs? To reconcile every best principle and tradition in a single system? Our answer is, 'Yes; **it's been done already**.' The New Testament tells us about Christ, that 'In him all the fullness of God was pleased to dwell, *and through him to reconcile to himself all things, whether on earth or in heaven, making peace by the blood of his cross.'*

One Man has done it. And he is big enough to hold the world together.

91. Am I a real disciple of Jesus?

How can I be sure that my faith is genuine, and that I won't turn out to be a fraud?

We do right to examine ourselves, to 'make your calling and election sure' (2 Peter 1:10). Here is a Trinitarian platform – not of smug arrogance, but of humble assurance. Having trusted Christ for salvation, how can I know that I'm a true believer?

1. The Word of God to us
It is God's unchanging Word – not my inner changeable feelings – that I must rely upon. Christ comes and knocks at the door of my life (Revelation 3:20). I respond to his dying love for me, and in thankful trust, invite him in. *Did he come in?*

'Er...well, I hope so! Um...I don't *feel* that he has come in!' But look again; it's a **promise**: 'If anyone hears my voice and opens the door, I **will** come in....' So did he come in? *Why, he must have. Because it says so!*

New believers do well to memorise other great statements of assurance – John 1:12; 5:24; 6:37; Romans 8:1; 1 John 5:11–13. Naturally, there is no room for complacency about our moral *state*. But about our *standing* – our position in God's sight – God does not want us to remain in doubt; *he has already transferred the believer into the kingdom of his Son* (Colossians 1:13,14). It says so!

2. The work of Christ for us
The Bible teaches us that at the Cross, the lifting of our guilt was *done*, so that we could be freed from the wrath of coming judgment, and be fully accepted by God, here and now (Romans 5:6–9).

Of course, we need *reminders* of this, for example at the service of Holy Communion (see chapter 36). To imagine that *we* could make any additional contribution to our salvation would be to insult Christ in his dying love. So test yourself: *Is it the death of Jesus that I am relying upon for my eternal salvation?* He has died for me, as a once and for all saving event. I don't have to do anything more.

3. The witness of the Spirit in us

'The Spirit himself bears witness with our spirit that we are children of God' (Romans 8:16). The Spirit does *in* us what Christ did *for* us, making Christ and his blessings real and personal (see chapter 88). Inwardly he confirms our position, as we begin to recognise that he really is working in us – in terms of a changed – and changing – life.

The true believer is only too aware of the power of indwelling sin (Romans 7:24) – *but we do know where the answer lies.* Learn the three 'tenses' of Salvation (end of chapter 30). And take in the words of John Newton, the converted slave trader: 'I am not what I ought to be; I am not what I wish to be; I am not what I hope to be; *but by the grace of God I am not what I was!'*

92. Can I lose my salvation?

Are there not indications in the Bible that believers can lose their salvation? Please see Hebrews 6.

Well, it looks like it at first:

> For it is impossible to restore again to repentance those who have once been enlightened, who have tasted the heavenly gift, and have shared in the Holy Spirit, and have tasted the goodness of the word of God and the power of the age to come, if they then fall away, since they are crucifying once again the Son of God to their own harm and holding him up to contempt (Hebrews 6:4-6 ESV).

A look at the context of this passage brings out the meaning. These were *Hebrew* members of the Christian church. The 'foundation' (vv.1,2) had already been laid for them in Old Testament Judaism – 'repentance', 'faith in God', 'washings', the 'laying on of hands', the doctrine of the 'resurrection' and 'eternal judgment' – *all of these were a valid part of Jewish teaching and practice.*

The problem of these worshippers was that because of the scriptural similarity between some of the 'foundational' Old Covenant practices and those of the New Covenant in Christ, they were easily tempted to revert to their former mindset *if they had never really trusted in Jesus from the start.* This is why it is no good 'once again' laying the foundation of the Old Testament; they *must* leave these elementary Old Testament doctrines of Christ and move on to 'maturity' (v.1), the full experience of life in Christ, if they are to have any hope.

None of the language here is that of Justification or the New Birth. If they had only been 'enlightened' (but not saved); if they had only 'tasted' and 'shared' (but not been transformed), then, humanly speaking it would be 'impossible' to win them over again, for by now they were 'inoculated' against the real thing.

It can happen today, when someone from a 'God-conscious' belief system makes an apparent transfer to Christianity. *It looks like a conversion.* They then revert to their former ways, and people wonder how they could have 'fallen away'. The more likely truth is that – during the time that they were joining in with Christian activities and worshipping the Christian 'God' – *they had never actually ceased worshipping their old deity.* The whole thing was a flirtation from start to finish.

Lapsed cynics will sometimes say, 'Christianity? I tried it once; it didn't work for me.' Were such 'tasters' ever really saved? Not if their lapse proves permanent. **'They went out from us, but they were not of us; for if they had been of us, they would have continued with us. But they went out, that it might become plain that they all are not of us'** (1 John 2:19 ESV).

Positively, it really seems that 'Once saved, always saved' (see chapter 91). Please look up John 6:37; 10:28,29; Hebrews 13:5. And plenty more. Can a believer be lost? *No – but don't experiment.*

93. I want to be holy, but I'm not!

Why am I not more effective in making a success of my life as a Christian? I sometimes despair over my slow rate of moral progress.

Let's know the difference between Justification (see chapter 29) and *Sanctification*. Many people never get this sorted.

Associated with 'sanctification' are 'saint', 'separation' and 'holy'. A *saint*, in New Testament terms is simply someone who has been 'set apart', or separated for God and for holiness. So, although Christians may often think of themselves as 'sinners', the New Testament never treats them as anything other than 'saints'. See how the apostle Paul addresses even the unruly church at Corinth:

> To the church of God that is at Corinth, to those sanctified in Christ Jesus, called to be saints... (1 Corinthians 1:2).

There are two ideas within the truth of sanctification. First, as a result of God's activity we are, 'in Christ', set aside for God and his service. It is a fact of Christian conversion. This is *positional sanctification*. It is instantaneous, along with justification. We may not feel like saints, but we **are** saints, from Day One.

Then, there is what may be called *conditional sanctification*. Those Corinthian believers were already 'sanctified' in Christ, but they were also called to *be* saints, to *become* holy. This is a process, conditional upon the Christian's use of God's means of grace, the Bible, prayer, the Church fellowship and the sacraments. On the whole it is as the *process,* that we normally think of sanctification.

Justification, then, is instantaneous – like the taking of a photograph. Sanctification is more like the processing of the film – as steadily, progressively, **we become more like Jesus in character**. Justification is when righteousness is *imputed* to a person – to chalk it up against our name. Sanctification is when righteousness is *imparted* to us, as – by the power of God's indwelling Spirit – we grow in faith and obedience. My colleague Rupert Higgins has said that it's the difference between getting married, as a *fact*, and becoming a good spouse, as a *process*.

So it is never going to be quick. No one is going to wake up one morning and declare, 'Well, I never; I've become holy!' **In fact, the sure-fire sign of the new birth in Christians, is that they are aware of their sins, and long to overcome them.** Look at Paul's words of testimony – *as an advanced believer* (Romans 7:24,25) – and take comfort! Awareness of sin is a healthy sign that we have turned around, and are now swimming *against* the current.

The power of indwelling sin, then, is not going to be *eradicated* by the Spirit's working. But it is going to be *counteracted*. We will be battling for holiness all our days.

Here is a fine apostolic prayer: **Now may the God of peace himself sanctify you completely, and may your whole spirit and soul and body be kept blameless at the coming of our Lord Jesus Christ. He who calls you is faithful; he will surely do it** *(1 Thessalonians 5:23,24)*.

94. What do I do when I am tempted?

I hear addresses on the power we are given to overcome our sins. But practically what should I do, when I face the Devil's pressures?

A little girl was asked in her Bible class what she did in the face of temptation. 'Well,' she replied, 'I send Jesus to the door.'

At that level, it was a very creditable reply. But it's really Christ who sends *us* to the door. Following Christ is not a passive affair. Notice the **active verbs** of the New Testament – 'wrestle' (Ephesians 6:12), 'fight' (1 Timothy 6:12), 'resist' (1 Peter 5:9), 'run' (Hebrews 12:1), 'flee' (2 Timothy 2:22).

The old Church of England Prayer Book has the phrase, to 'beat down Satan under our feet'.

Before Christ's Spirit entered our life, we couldn't really do battle at all. We were like prisoners, bound by guilt; by the ropes of sins and habits that were taking us to hell. So helpless were we, that we weren't even aware that we *were* prisoners.

Then one day the picture changed. Someone had been praying for us. A colleague had built a bridge of friendship into our lives, *and Christ walked over the bridge*. He came into the house of our lives, sliced through the bonds that held us prisoner, and threw them into a bin. He picked up a baseball bat in the corner, and said, 'See that intruder at the door? Take this and go and deal with him'.

We shrink back. 'O great Liberator, can't *you* go?'

'No, no. I've already dealt with him 2,000 years ago; he knows he's a beaten enemy. Now it's your turn to give him the push.'

And that, frankly is what we do. When the Liberator comes, he doesn't set us free *from* the fight. He sets us free *for* the fight. So, faced by pressure and temptation, *we are to choose not to sin*. It is as simple – and as inconvenient – as that. The Devil – and he is a person (chapter 6) – has power, but his is a limited power against the person indwelt by the Spirit of Christ (1 John 4:4). He cannot make a believer sin; he only has power to entice and tempt. *If we do wrong, it is we who choose to do so.*

We don't have to look for a new massive infusion of spiritual power. All the power we needed was given us, when Christ entered our life. What we do frequently lack is not power, but *motivation*. Half the time we don't even want to win; it is too personally inconvenient!

Answer: Raise the motivation. We do this by gaining such a conception of Christ, once crucified, now raised, ascended – and finally returning in dazzling glory – that we *want* to win! *Start* every day with the Bible. *Ask* every day that you may be filled with the Spirit. *Dedicate* yourself, every day, as Christ's faithful servant – and fighter! *Meet* regularly with the friends of Jesus around the Bible. And then *expect* to win.

95. Why should Christians suffer?

Why is it that following Jesus seems in many quarters to be so unpopular? Is it inevitable that we must suffer as Christians?

Yes, it is. A Bible sentence to remember is Acts 14:22, where we read that Paul and Barnabas were 'strengthening the souls of the disciples...and saying that **through many tribulations we must enter the kingdom of God'**.

Once we are alert to this truth of essential Christian experience, we find it everywhere – and then we wonder that we didn't see it before.

'Tribulations'
The Greek word is *thlipsis*...It describes a confining, squeezing pressure. It describes 'affliction' (James 1:27), material shortages (2 Corinthians 8:13), and a woman's labour pains (John 16:21). It's used extensively of Christian suffering (2 Corinthians 2:4; 1 Peter 1:6). All down history the Christian church has faced the squeezing of numerous adversaries. The expectation is that if we choose the way of Christ, life will be made uncomfortable. This needs to be taught to new believers.

'Must'
The *must* of Acts 14:22 is the Greek 'must' of **necessity**. The indication is that 'tribulation' is an essential component of following Jesus. 'In the world', said Jesus, 'you will have tribulation [*thlipsis*].' There are two reasons for this; first, because we are called to follow a Man who was himself called upon to suffer. It is for his Name's sake that we do so (Matthew 24:9; Luke 22:28,29).

Secondly, God has chosen the way of tribulation for our spiritual growth (Romans 5:3). Naturally we tend to see adversity as an unnecessary interruption – and we hope that later we can get back to living a 'normal Christian life'. Then we discover that adversity *is* the normal Christian life; it signals the 'nearness' of God's kingdom (Luke 21:25-28,31). The apostle Peter emphasises the Cross as an integral way of life for the believer (1 Peter 4:1,12,13).

'Enter'
The Christian and the unbelieving world see adversity from opposite poles. To the world, suffering is a dead end. To the Christian, it is a gateway into personal growth and the very life of the kingdom. Strangely and uniquely the Christian revelation sees 'suffering' and 'glory' as belonging together (1 Peter 5:1,10). The whole of Paul's two letters to the Corinthians is on the theme of *power through weakness*. The reason is that the Cross, in its apparent weakness, possesses the greatest power in all history.

'The Kingdom of God'
The kingdom is not land. It is the rule of God through the appointed king, Jesus Christ, in the lives of his subjects, world-wide. It runs parallel to all that is implied by *salvation*. 'The Kingdom of God is not a matter of eating and drinking **but of righteousness and peace and joy in the Holy Spirit'** (Romans 14:17).

What an enigma. We need not seek suffering; yet suffering and the kingdom do go together (Revelation 1:9). *Where does the magnetism lie?* Why, in the Man of Galilee who beckons us and says, 'I've been this way myself. Take up your cross and follow me.' And millions have.

FOR FURTHER STUDY: Richard Bewes, *The Stone that Became a Mountain*, Christian Focus (See Chapter 9)

96. How important is baptism?

Having become a Christian from another religion, I am nervous about the prospect of baptism. It could be a tension point as far as my family is concerned. How vital is it to be baptised?

First, welcome to the family of the Lord Jesus Christ. Every day, some 100,000 people become his followers, and every week some 1,600 new congregations come into being. This is a great landmark for you at such a point in history!

But, while the greatest problems – of your forgiveness, your relationship to God and your eternal destiny – were all solved the day you turned to Christ, there will naturally be a whole bundle of new problems facing you. Others, who are now your sisters and brothers in Jesus Christ, feel for you and no doubt will pray for you. Here are my words of reassurance, as you weigh up the matter of baptism:

1. Christ has already saved you
Our salvation does not depend on whether we have been baptised – or we would immediately be into a religion of salvation by deeds. It is the saving death of Jesus that has done it all – and his 'Baptism of the Spirit' brought you into the company of all believers the day you were converted (1 Corinthians 12:13). The day we say 'Yes' to Christ, we are as assured of a place by his side, eternally, as the thief on the Cross.

2. Christ is going to keep you
Having taken the great step of trusting Christ, you can take heart from the words of the apostle Peter to the persecuted believers of his time. He saw them as *'kept by the power of God through faith, unto salvation ready to be revealed in the last time'* (1 Peter 1:5 KJV). When the Lord Jesus Christ comes into our lives, he is not going to forget us. And here is his

encouragement if baptism looks like becoming a possibility: 'Fear not, therefore; you are of more value than many sparrows. So everyone who acknowledges me before men, I also will acknowledge before my Father who is in heaven' (Matthew 10:31,32).

3. Christ is going to guide you

I'm sure you are in prayer about the question of baptism. You can relax over this issue. The Lord knows about the timing and feasibility of taking this step. It is good to stay in touch with the leaders of your Christian fellowship. As you and they pray, you will surely feel settled eventually as to what Christ is saying to you.

4. Christ is going to use you

A new thing has happened. Because Christ has come into your life, *you* are now the key person, spiritually, in your family. We can certainly believe that from now on, through your prayers, your own testimony of a changed life – and perhaps one day through your baptism – others too in your family will be enabled to turn to him who is 'the way, the truth and the life'.

My closing word of encouragement for you – Proverbs 16:7.

97. Why join a local church?

I am a very new Christian. I sense that I should join a church. But which? Please give me some advice.

It is wonderful to greet you. Wherever you go, you are a member of the biggest family of belief ever known; it is the *only* group to which Jesus Christ has personally pledged himself.

You are right to be thinking about 'the church'; those 'called out and summoned together' under the headship of Christ. The church is not a building as such, it is a divine company:

> But you are a chosen people, a royal priesthood, a holy nation, a people belonging to God, that you may declare the praises of him who called you out of darkness into his wonderful light (1 Peter 2:9 NIV).

The church, then, is to be the biggest thing in our life. Our membership within 'the Body of Christ' (to use one Bible metaphor of the church) is going to colour and enhance all of our relationships, work, recreation and plans. Naturally, this means that we need to discover which local manifestation of the church Christ is calling us to join. Pray about it.

Here are the questions to ask as you consider joining a church:

1. Does the Bible actually get opened here?

Try and find a church that really does take the Scriptures seriously, and preaches through them. Does it have small classes or groups that help enquirers and new believers? At our own church we have a helpful course – now internationally–developed – entitled *Christianity Explored* (www.christianityexplored.com). It is equipped with handbooks and videos as required. *Basically it is a Bible diet that you are looking for.*

2. Is this the kind of church you could take an uncommitted friend to?

A vital question! It need not matter overmuch whether the church is lively or quiet, big or small, traditional or modern....*but is it real?* Is there an ease and warmth of spirit present? If so, then it is likely to be a praying church. Would you feel ashamed, taking a friend along? Are they likely to hear a message that will help and challenge them?

3. Is there a recognisably New Testament feel to the church?

Is it Trinitarian in its emphasis on Father, Son and Holy Spirit as equally God? Is the saving death of Christ at its centre (1 Corinthians 2:2)? Do the hymns reflect this? Are baptism and the Lord's Supper (the Holy Communion) a proper part of the church order (the two 'sacraments' instituted by Jesus)?

4. On the whole, are the arrows pointing outwards from the church?

A Gospel fellowship will always be reaching out, with the good news of Christ, service of others in the community and involvement in worldwide mission. *Look for the meeting dedicated to intercession and prayer* – that is always a dead give-away, as to where the ministry is directed.

We will never find a perfect church – simply because every church is composed of individuals like us. But Christ loves the church, and so must we.

98. Why are Christians a problem?

I have to tell you that I find non-Christian acquaintances easier to get on with than my fellow-believers. Why is it that so often the non-Christians are nicer, more hard-working and even more honest than the Christians?

This really hurts. I'm afraid there is a precedent for such a pattern. Writing to the Christians at Corinth, Paul was aware of their poor standards. God was undoubtedly in their lives; they could boast of spiritual abilities, including speaking in tongues; yet they were grouped around rival factions (3:4,21), they were spiritually conceited (4:6–21), they accommodated sexual immorality (5:1,2), they took each other to court (6:1–8)....and they failed over apostleship, marriage, women, money – and even the Holy Communion.

Paul wrote, 'I could not address you as spiritual, but as worldly – mere infants in Christ' (3:1). Again, 'You are still worldly. For since there is jealousy and quarrelling among you, are you not worldly? Are you not acting like mere men?' (3:3).

That is the scandal – supposed followers of the purest Person who ever lived, yet acting like 'mere men'.
But be thankful that we possess the Corinthian correspondence, because it demonstrates what an unpleasant bunch of people Christians can be when they (we?) have barely begun to experience the sanctifying work of the Holy Spirit. Many of those among the Corinthians had been *sexually immoral, idolaters, adulterers, men who practised homosexuality, thieves, greedy, drunkards, revilers and swindlers* (1 Corinthians 6:10). 'Such', Paul continues, **'were some of you'.**

Where were the 'nice' people that you mention? Presumably still outside the church; they sensed no need of salvation! Nice people are probably born nice – it's no credit to them. It certainly doesn't take away the fact of their rejection of God and their need of salvation.

In almost any church we join, we shall be aware of the grumblers and the trouble-makers, the prickly and the angular, the mean and the avaricious. Indeed, no true New Testament church can possibly be completely pure – *would we even want it that way?* It is always a healthy sign of evangelistic involvement in the community, when a church has an untidy, and even unruly, 'fringe membership'. Better that, than to have a church which is ultra-pure – *and well quarantined from outside influences.*

My challenge is this. Get into a house group or similar gathering organised by the church. For it's right there, in the enclosed confines of a small group, that we can really put into practice the New Testament principles of living as the church: **'Put on then, as God's chosen ones, holy and beloved, compassion, kindness, humility, meekness and patience, bearing with one another and, if one has a complaint against another, forgiving each other; as the Lord has forgiven you, so you also must forgive. And above all these put on love, which binds everything together in perfect harmony'** (Colossians 3:12–14).

You can't really do *that* on a Sunday. It's the small group which is the workshop of practical Christianity.

99. How to help the unbeliever?

How do I help the friend who says that he would like to believe, but that he simply can't?

Your friend's brightest prospect of becoming a believer in Christ may well rest, humanly speaking, on you. Nearly every time an individual responds to the good news of Jesus, somewhere in the background there was a friend. As Augustine said sixteen centuries ago, 'One loving spirit sets another on fire'.

Let us open this up a little.

1. Faith needs a backcloth
In the days of the New Testament, the backcloth was the Jewish tradition, stretching back over centuries – and the common expectation of a Messiah. Today it is rather different. Your friend may not have a religious framework for his thinking; alternatively he may have a distorted religious world-view, such as is found in New Age.

A little undermining of his presuppositions will be necessary – and because you are his friend, it can be done without offence. An obvious opener is the challenge, 'Describe to me your world-view'. For every man, woman and child on Planet Earth has a world-view; that is, believes something about the meaning of life as they find it. What is his? Explore it, probe it, question it and undermine it – and all the time you are praying, *Make him hungry, Lord.*

2. Faith needs an event
We know, of course, that the search for faith is not a blind, empty search for *anything*. It's more like the ancient search for the source of the River Nile. Everybody knew that there must be a great reservoir that was feeding the mighty river; it was only a question of persevering.

In the Christian context we have been given the latitude and longitude for the search for ultimate reality. We need look no further than the life, death and resurrection of the world's pivotal figure, Jesus Christ. In your discussions, keep coming back to *him*. The road to a living faith is the road that keeps Christ in view. 'Faith', wrote Os Guinness, 'does not feed on thin air, but on facts' (*Doubt,* Lion Publishing).

In the end, faith, for your friend, is not going to be a 'feeling' about Christianity, but a rational and willing **response**.

3. Faith needs a trigger

'Who do you say that I am?' Jesus asked Peter. It was a trigger moment for the disciple. But a trigger can equally be an event, an illness, the birth of a baby, a visit to church, the reading of a book. Keep looking for those opportunities that may help to tip your friend towards the Kingdom.

It can take a while, going about it as the singer Garth Hewitt once declared to a journalist, when he said, *'My role is that of creating doubt in the mind of the ardent unbeliever'*. But when that job is done, the way is created for the electric 'trigger' moment.

Lord....make him hungry.

FOR FURTHER STUDY: Rico Tice and Barry Cooper, *Christianity Explored,* Paternoster Press.

100. Can I be a global Christian?

As a Christian, I have a job that takes me all over the world. I do have a church at home, but I cannot always be there. Your advice please.

You are so right in having your own church back at home. There is no reason why you should not be in a home group or church Bible class. If you are going to be away, you can always ring up the leaders and give them your prayer requests – and ask them for theirs. *Take membership seriously.*

It is a wonderful thing that has happened to you; you have joined not some cosy club, but the world kingdom and church inaugurated by none other than Jesus Christ....**and you are a travelling ambassador for this outfit**.

Yours is a privilege that does not come to many of us. Of course there is the high priority of your professional work to consider – but if you take a little care over it, you can also be a missionary. Sports coaches make good missionaries in other countries – and no less do business people. I know several such.

The concern expressed in your question is a right one; it would be so easy to let all the ropes of your discipleship and church life slacken little by little. But this need not be so. Carry that Bible on your person into every day – and even if prayer is happening at strange times of day, let it be little and often.

Build up an international dossier of Christian contacts and churches, worldwide. Slowly it can come together if you work at it. Gradually you can find your way around the Family of Christ on different continents; building up the names and addresses of people whom you can count on for fellowship, perhaps some Bible study, and prayer support.

Become an international ambassador to these many contacts. How can you encourage *them*? What of the overseas churches that you visit – what are their pastors short of? Can you take a little supply along? Some book gifts in your brief case; a few bars of soap; some tapes of Bible addresses? Eventually it could be that your overseas visits will be eagerly looked forward to at the other end.

I once travelled with such a man. He knew the names of the children, in the families he dropped in on. He would pick them up and give them a hug – and then have a tiny present for them. He would remember their news, *because he wrote everything down.*

Begin as an international intercessor

Names, contacts, churches, problems; turn them into prayer as you travel. And see if, from time to time, you can report in to your home group when you return. And might you have something to bring back for *them* too? Yours is a privileged role. God bless you in it. And don't forget your toothbrush!

50 DIFFICULT BIBLE PASSAGE QUESTIONS

The hill, though high, I covet to ascend,
The difficulty will not me offend;
For I perceive the way to life lies here:
Come, pluck up heart, let's neither faint nor fear;
Better, tho' *difficult*, the right way to go,
Than wrong, though *easy*, where the end is woe.

(John Bunyan, 1628–1688: *The Pilgrim's Progress*)

In this final section of the book, we will touch on some of the obvious – the 'top' – difficult Bible questions. **We will take them in strict Biblical order**. And because we cannot cover them all, one of our aims should be to try and identify the **principles** with which to approach these passages – and so equip ourselves better for other and future challenges. *This section can be used as real Bible study, as Scripture references are carefully looked up and read.*

Make me hungry is the prayer. And for those others with whom we would wish to share our discoveries? *Make them hungry*. And further, for those with whom we meet at those business breakfast Bible studies, those student seminars, those video sessions with 'Open Home, Open Bible', 'Book by Book' – and all the rest?

Make us hungry!

1. Genesis 1 – Six 'days' of Creation?

Are we now to understand the days of Creation in the light of scientific advance?

Certainly not. Science is inevitably an ever-changing, ever-switching discipline. Theories that held sway during one decade are challenged and disproved in the next. By contrast, the Bible's account of Creation has stood through all of history (see chapter 3). Millions of modern readers accept and are inspired by Genesis 1 just as much as the ancient peoples were.

'Days' we can all understand. They are built into the whole rhythm of our existence – with the significant repeated phrase of Genesis 1, *and there was evening and there was morning – one day.* The 'seventh day' of rest is also emphasised – this resulting in the creation principle of the one **day** in seven that features in the Ten Commandments.

'If', as Derek Kidner writes, 'the "days" were not days at all, would God have countenanced the word? Does he trade in inaccuracies, however edifying?' (*Genesis,* Tyndale Press, 1967).

Stick with *days.* Naturally the Creator had his own way of shaping and measuring a 'day' in the momentous dawn of our human story. But once we make Genesis match with scientific findings of the present, **there would be a mismatch ten years down the road**, because science, unlike Genesis, would have moved on elsewhere by then.

2. Genesis 2:7 – Can evolution be accommodated?

'*The Lord God formed the man from the dust of the ground and breathed into his nostrils the breath of life and the man became a living being.*' Could this imply an evolutionary process?

Evolution? It has proved to be a largely sterile debate over the past 100 years and more. Genesis 2:7, while not disallowing an element of evolution (see Job 10:8,9) – nevertheless must be allowed to make its **own** point, namely, that – in physical terms – we derive from the very *materials* that make up this earth and its contents. It needs to be balanced by Genesis 1:27 that tells us of the *image of God* in which we have been made. The two statements complement each other, and stand for ever, irrespective of how evolutionary theories themselves may develop.

Bible students, with a reverent regard for Genesis 1 and 2, can be found on both sides of the evolution divide. Where the main problem lies is in the evolutionists' view of death as the creative engine in natural selection, rather than as an intruder – which is how the Bible presents it. This obviously has to be taken account of in any debate.

What unites us, of course, is our common belief in an original creation, and the truth that the whole human race comes from a single stock (Acts 17:26). **Our past mistake has been in spending fruitless hours *defending* a position, rather than in *proclaiming* the massive truth – that men and women are not simply collections of biochemical reactions. We have been brought into this world as god-like beings – made for eternal fellowship with the Creator!**

3. Genesis 4:14 – Other populations than Adam's?

Cain – on his banishment to be a wanderer on earth, following his murder of Abel – laments, *'whoever finds me will kill me'*. Doesn't this indicate other early populations on earth, besides Adam's?

Different explanations have been suggested. Some have thought that the 'killers' might be wild animals rather than people; others that Adam's creation was not that of Genesis 1:27, but was of the highest type of the human race, and had been preceded by the production of inferior races, now widely scattered. Yet others suggest populations of the *future* that might threaten Cain.

But the most natural explanation is that Cain's fears were groundless. He was not to know for sure that no one else existed but Adam and his family; that there were not other clans in the unfamiliar regions to which he was being banished – people like himself who could be prone to violence. Thus the sign and promise that God gives Cain is a gracious accommodation of the fugitive in his ignorant fears.

4. Genesis 4:17 – Who was Cain's wife?

With Cain and Abel as the two brothers – and there being no other peoples outside Adam's family – how was it, then, that Cain, on being banished to the land of Nod, finds a wife there? Who was she?

It is an old favourite, flung by hecklers – even today – at open-air preachers. Of course there is an answer. But the last time I was asked this, I held back my answer, by replying, 'How serious are you in asking this?' Then, 'How would it change your attitude to Christianity if there was an answer?' Then finally, 'If I give you an answer to your intellectual satisfaction, will you become a Christian tonight?'

Scenting danger, my inquisitor began to wobble. Perhaps it was partly because his bluff had been called that he actually became a Christian that very night.

The answer is twofold. First, we do not read that Cain **found** himself a wife in the land of Nod. Rather, it was there that Cain 'lay with' his wife, who then gave birth to Enoch (Genesis 4:17). Secondly, although Cain and Abel were but two brothers initially, there were also to be 'other sons and daughters' fathered by Adam in his long life (Genesis 5:4). Cain would have married one of these daughters, when necessity demanded some intermarrying at a time when the race had yet to increase.

5. Genesis 6:1–4 – Marrying with angels?

The passage reads as though angelic beings ('sons of God') were marrying humans. What is the point of this account?

Some have certainly so interpreted the passage, appealing to Jude 6,7 and 2 Peter 2:4–6. But then angels neither marry nor are given in marriage (Matthew 22:30). *Perhaps we are wiser to look to the immediate context of this passage*, for Genesis 5 ends with a detailed ancestral line – 'the book of the generations of Adam' (Genesis 5:1).

As we get into chapter 6, an unwelcome departure from the chosen line becomes apparent, with some of its daughters becoming ensnared in alien relationships with the 'sons of God'. Who are they? The term can describe high-ranking, though worthless, young men: **'I said, "you are gods, sons of the Most High, all of you"'** (Psalm 82:6). Here intermarriage seems to be taking place between women from the pure line of Seth (Genesis 5:3f) and the licentious high ranking men from the expelled line of Cain, the *Nephilim*, known for their physical size (Numbers 13:33).

This chapter, then, shows human rebellion to be spiralling out of control ('My Spirit will not contend with man for ever' v.3). The direct result is the judgment of the Flood.

6. Genesis 11:5–7 – Does God feel threatened?

'If....they have begun to do this, then nothing they plan to do will be impossible for them. Come, let us go down and confuse their language....' This reads like the panic action of a threatened tyrant, but surely God is not like this?

God's reaction to the building of the Tower of Babel has sometimes been dismissed by the cynics in just such a way. But no. *These are not the words of a petty demagogue fearing a rival.* After all, the Lord God had, at the Creation, deliberately set the world under the care and guardianship of men and women.

Rather, here are words that express the concern, reminiscent of Luke 23:31, of a caring father for his wayward children. The warning from Babel – the world's first real glimpse of secular humanism – was this: *Let the unfettered energies of fallen human beings become combined and who knows where the limits will be, in the evil and destruction that they could unitedly unleash upon the earth?*

For this reason a restraint is placed upon the human race, in terms of a scattering of peoples, cultures and languages. From now on it would be impossible for one evil person or nation to exercise unlimited power, without being counteracted by another. The lesson of Babel is that – desirable though it is to work together – if we leave God out of the planning (as, for example, the United Nations studiously does), frustration and fragmentation will be the result.

7. Genesis 16:11,12 – Ishmael's blessing?

How does the blessing that Ishmael received fit in with that of Abraham, Isaac and Jacob?

The New Testament takes into account the birth of Ishmael, from whom Arabs today claim their descent – and describes him as **'born after the flesh'** (Galatians 4:22,23 KJV). Isaac, his half-brother – the true and intended heir of the Covenant – is declared to be born **'by promise'**. That is the basic contrast between these two children of Abraham.

Ishmael was born to Hagar, as a result of a failure in patience on Abraham's part (Genesis 16). This is why the apostle Paul draws the analogy between the two boys; Ishmael is equated with self-made religion; Isaac with that of the Spirit (Galatians 4:29).

Ishmael's birth is indeed accompanied by a divinely pronounced blessing. His descendants 'will be too numerous to count'; he would be the father of twelve princes, and from him would arise a great nation (Genesis 16:10–12; 17:20). But there is nothing here about a promised land, of future blessing for the world through him, of God's eternal Covenant or of the message of salvation. Ishmael's, unlike Isaac's, was to be a temporal blessing only and would not be a vehicle of the Gospel.

8. Genesis 22 – Why sacrifice Isaac?

Does God's ordering of the sacrifice of Isaac somewhat resemble the idle experiment of a psychopath – to see how far one of his followers would go in his obedience?

No, that would be to turn the episode on its head. Genesis 22 is an enduring prototype of *the Gospel*. The central character is not Abraham, but the God of grace and provision. Abraham never calls the locality 'the Place of Testing', but rather *Jehovah Jireh* – 'The Lord will Provide' (Genesis 22:14).

By now, Abraham knows the ways and the voice of God – so he trusts him. **Of course God is going to fulfil his promise of blessing to the world through Isaac.** Abraham is not lying when he tells the servants that he and Isaac are going to 'worship', *and that they will be coming back.* Hebrews 11:19 comments, 'He considered that God was able to raise men even from the dead.'

Thus, when Isaac asks where is the lamb for the sacrifice, it is with complete confidence that his father answers, 'God himself will provide a lamb.' *The substitute for Isaac – 'the ram caught in a thicket' – wasn't the real, the ultimate substitute.* Centuries later, John the Baptist, on seeing Jesus, would exclaim, 'Behold the Lamb of God, who takes away the sin of the world!' (John 1:29). Here in Christ was God's all-time self-offering of grace and love. The wonder of Genesis 22 lies in Jesus' words, 'Your father Abraham rejoiced to see **my day**; he saw it, and was glad' (John 8:56). The sacrifice of Isaac was one of the earliest real curtain-raisers to the Cross of Jesus Christ!

9. Genesis 30–32 – The speckled goats?

Jacob's reliance on visual images as a breeding process, affecting the unborn embryos of sheep and goats, reads like legendary superstition. How can such an action be a legitimate part of the Bible?

It's as much a part of the Bible as King Saul's superstitious reliance on a medium for his guidance (1 Samuel 28). Not everything in the Bible is there for God's endorsement. Jacob's actions in these chapters are hardly worthy of a man who had been selected for blessing. In his character he is still suspicious, revengeful, shifty – and superstitious as well.

Yet it seems, by the end of Genesis 30, that the breeding device used against his crooked uncle, Laban, is remarkably successful! The credit appears to be Jacob's. But there was another side to it. **Always look beyond the Bible's chapter divisions – which are not a part of the original text.** For in chapter 31:12,13, Jacob has the grace to ascribe the real turn-around in his fortunes to *God's action*, revealed to him in a dream. He needn't have gone to all the trouble with the absurd breeding programme. God wanted him blessed anyway – and back in his own country!

10. Exodus 4:21 – Unfair on Pharaoh?

I feel sorry for Pharaoh, faced by Moses and the plagues of Egypt. Why did God 'harden Pharaoh's heart' so that he could not repent?

Don't spend too much pity on the man. Pharaoh wanted respite from the plagues, *but he didn't want to let go*. No dictators ever do! The Pharaohs and the Caesars, yes and the Hitlers, Stalins, Pol Pots, Amins and the various terrorist consortia of our time, tend to leave history without ever repenting. The disasters of Revelation 8 and 9 are like warning trumpets: 'Repent!' But Revelation 9:20 sums it up, 'They still did not repent'. As they live, so they die.

Pharaoh is given his chance ten times over. But from the beginning God knew what would happen. Every time Pharaoh hardened his heart against the revealed truth of God's message, it was a further tightening of the noose upon him. If people deliberately choose to pursue error, 'God sends them a powerful delusion, so that they will believe the lie' (2 Thessalonians 2:11; see also Romans 1: 24,26,28). This is the pattern in every era. *Where is your heart?* That is the key question for every person in this world.

11. Exodus 4:24 – God attacking Moses?

Why, on Moses' way to Egypt, did the Lord seek to put him to death? It seems a strange way for God to act towards his follower.

It does. But how closely *was* Moses following the Lord? Verses 24 and 25 reveal that, despite his obedience to the call to lead Israel out of Egypt, Moses had omitted to circumcise his son Gershom – born to his Midianite wife, Zipporah. And any uncircumcised male was regarded as having broken God's Covenant, and should be removed from God's people (Genesis 17:9–14).

This explains the episode. Here is Moses, disobeying God within his family, at the outset of a mighty enterprise. If disobedience was to be tolerated at the start – and this by the leader – what hope was there for the remainder of the operation? Presumably Moses fell ill and nearly died. Zipporah gets the message, and herself performs the rite of circumcision on Gershom. At that point, Moses recovers.

Even God's friends are not exempt from his actions of judgment; indeed judgment may well *start* with them (1 Peter 4:17). Moses needed to learn that, in the great adventure that lay ahead, God was quite prepared to do without him altogether....if necessary.

12. Exodus 20:4 – No images, no art?

I have been told by devotees of other religions that if paintings or carvings of human beings or any other creatures are made, then we Christians are disobeying our own commandments. Is this true?

The text reads, 'You shall not make yourself a graven image, or any likeness of anything that is in heaven above, or that is in the earth beneath, or that is in the water under the earth' (Exodus 20:4 RSV).

I have noticed that when that sentence is quoted to Christian people, the words that follow are invariably left out: *You shall not bow down to them or serve them.* The whole context of the second commandment is one of worship, and the issue is that of idolatry. Is this a forbidding of art in general? No, it is not. We have only to read on – to Exodus 25:18 and God's own instructions for the forming of the cherubim of gold – placed in the most sacred part of the worship tent (see also Exodus 35:30-35). Of course, created figures like that were not to be worshipped; they were there for adornment – and sometimes to make a teaching point.

This accepted, the fallenness of our human natures always leaves us open to idolatry, whether of metal or mental images. Israel learnt it the hard way. We must learn from Israel.

13. Exodus 20:5 – Generational guilt?

I wonder about the fairness of the Lord visiting the iniquity of the fathers upon the children of the third and fourth generations.

The fact is, God's basic human unit is *the Family*. All of the Old Testament is about the story of a family. And although it is true that ultimately we must all bear the responsibility of our own sin (Deuteronomy 24:16; Ezekiel 18:4), we can still recognise the principle of Exodus 20:5 as a pattern affecting all human life.

Children, and even remote descendants are liable to inherit, not so much the *penalties* of their forebears' sins, but rather their *consequences* – in terms of disease, poverty, education and lifestyle (see Leviticus 26:39).

But we are not at the mercy of impersonal deterministic forces. It does not follow that if your parents or grandparents lived in an unprincipled way, you are inevitably doomed to an unstable or purposeless life. Preaching, witness and intercessory prayer can turn the tables for *anyone*. When this happens, the lone believer in the ancestral line becomes the key figure for the whole family. Such is the power of God's Word and Spirit.

14. Exodus 26:34 – A flat contradiction?

The regulations of Exodus 26: 34, 35 for the ordering of the Tabernacle tent of meeting, placed the ark of the Covenant in 'The Most Holy Place' on its own – while the golden altar of incense was to be placed, with the table and lampstand, in the adjoining 'Holy Place'. But in the New Testament, Hebrews 9:4 states that the Most Holy Place *'had the golden altar of incense and the gold-covered ark of the covenant.'* What are we to make of this clear Bible contradiction?

Look at the context. Pray for light. A little Greek can help. Turn to Hebrews 9:4, and look up the word **'had'** in a Greek lexicon. It can mean 'hold', 'contain' or 'possess' – as later in v.4 ('a golden urn *holding* the manna'). But there is another use of the word – which bears the sense of 'including', 'connecting', or 'associated with' (as in Hebrews 6:9) *'things that* **belong** *to salvation'* (RSV, ESV). It is this usage which features in the text before us.

Were there then certain conditions, when the golden censer could be said to 'belong to', or 'be associated with', the ark in the Most Holy Place? Yes, there were, particularly on the Day of Atonement – *which is the very context of Hebrews 9* (see v.7). On the Day of Atonement, the altar of incense was included with the mercy seat of the ark in a very significant way. First, the blood of the sin-offering was sprinkled on *both of them* (Leviticus 16:15-19). Secondly, a censer from the golden altar was to be taken *'inside the veil'* (that is, into the Most Holy Place – Leviticus 16:12). Despite the separating curtain then, these two sacred articles of furniture were indeed very closely connected (see Exodus 40:5).

The final clincher to the link between the golden altar of incense and the Most Holy Place, is in 1 Kings 6:22, where King Solomon is recorded as furnishing the Temple – the successor to the former Tabernacle: 'Also the whole altar **that belonged to the inner sanctuary** he overlaid with gold.'

Thus there is no Bible contradiction between Exodus and Hebrews. All that was needed was some patient Bible study.

15. Leviticus – An enjoyable read?

There are no stories in Leviticus. Instead 27 interminable chapters on rites, sacrifices and ceremonial procedure. Is there help available?

Let's *make* it a story. The book of Leviticus and the Gospel of the Lord Jesus Christ make up a story of two lenses.

There are two cameras that I own – and love. One I am using a great deal of the time; it's modern and easy to use. It takes great pictures. The other is older than I am; it's a little, battered aluminium Vest Pocket Kodak. Though the two cameras are well separated in years, they both have the same function. If I point them at some object, *they will both take the same picture*. True, the VPK won't take pictures with quite the same clarity as its modern counterpart. Nevertheless, *out* of those older cameras were developed the later models – and on the same principles.

The story of two lenses. That's *Leviticus* – and the New Testament *Gospels*. Leviticus is BC. The Gospels – and letters like Hebrews and 1 Peter – are AD. Leviticus gave God's people an understanding of the Lord in his holiness – and how it could ever be possible to approach him. It was the way of blood, and death, and sacrifice. *Here was an education*, preparing us for the way of the Cross. Same lens, same principle: **Without the shedding of blood there is no forgiveness of sins** (Hebrews 9:22). And that is the Gospel of the Bible, from cover to cover.

You will come to love Leviticus. Take it in big chunks, to start with. And as you read it, murmur to yourself, *'This was **the** evangelistic book for our Jewish forebears. It meant life to them'*.

16. Numbers 22:28 – A talking donkey?

I do believe in the authority of the Bible, but I cannot understand the account of Balaam's donkey. Are we really to understand that it used human words to speak to Balaam?

Yes, we are! It's true that an awful lot of scholars try to wriggle out of it, but you can't ignore the statement of that most ancient of all commentators, the apostle Peter himself – 'a speechless donkey spoke with human voice, and restrained the prophet's madness' (2 Peter 2:16).

If we read the whole passage in Numbers 22, it begins to come together. Whether the voice was heard only by Balaam is not certain. But these points are clear.

The communication originated with God, not with the donkey. 'Then the Lord opened the mouth of the donkey' (v.28). Balaam was riding along, out of harmony with God's will for his life. He was noted for his great powers of oratory – and the irony is that he was stopped in his tracks by the message of a donkey.

Why a donkey? Surely because of the contrast. The donkey saw the angel blocking the way ahead, before Balaam ever did, and so exercised more spiritual discernment than the supposed mighty leader. How are the mighty fallen! The Bible has never forgotten Balaam (Jude 11, Revelation 2:14). The emphasis is on the comparison between a man of reputedly great spiritual utterance, and a common little donkey. So great is the degree to which the hardening process can set in.

17. Deuteronomy 4:19 – Paganism OK?

Please explain the words, 'when you....see the sun, moon and stars...do not be enticed into bowing down to them and worshipping *things the Lord your God has apportioned to all the nations under heaven*'.

If it looks difficult at first sight, we must remember the certain fact that the Lord God simply did not tolerate rival deities – in any shape or form. Only one Person is to be worshipped.

But we also know that Israel was a nation set apart to reflect the truth and message of God to the surrounding heathen nations. God's people were not to live like the heathen, or to pray like them. The worship of the sun, moon and stars? *That's for heathen people!* A slightly similar expression is in Matthew 6:32, where Jesus warns against materialism, and says, 'For the pagans run after all *these* things'.

So we are to understand Deuteronomy 4:19. The stress is on the fact that the worship of Nature is only for the heathen – that's *their* province as far as God is concerned.

18. Deuteronomy 7:1–3 – Show no mercy?

God's commands to Israel, to obliterate the nations in Canaan, sounds like a nationalistic programme of ethnic genocide. How can we escape coming to this conclusion?

By paying attention to the big picture; to the Bible truth of Salvation. The 'Promised Land', so prominent in the book of Deuteronomy, is far more than a strip of territory bordering the Mediterranean. As Abraham himself knew (Hebrews 11:13–16), 'the land' stood for, and pointed to, all that believers are promised in the Gospel, right up to their inheritance in the new heaven and the new earth, brought in at Christ's return.

On the opposite side of Salvation is Judgment, of which the Scriptures repeatedly warn through numerous 'pre-runs', from the Flood onwards. Here is one such, in Deuteronomy 7. Israel is the instrument of divine judgment brought upon seven godless nations descended from Canaan (son of the degenerate Ham – Genesis 9:22–27). Sexual depravity and child sacrifice characterised their terrible lifestyles.

Deuteronomy 7 is concerned with spiritual, not ethnic issues. In any case, Israel itself was, by now, wider than a single ethnic strand. A 'mixed multitude' had joined the great exodus from Egypt (Exodus 12:38). Indeed, the alien Hivites themselves (who later became the Gibeonites) threw in their lot with Israel, and so escaped destruction, becoming eventually absorbed into the people of God, and even being defended by them (Joshua 9:7,15; 10:1, 2, 6–8).

When judgment comes, the time for 'mercy' is over. The Amorites, for example (v.1) had been given hundreds of years to mend their ways, ever since their escalating sins had found mention in Genesis 15:16. Their time had now run out – as will that of every man and woman in the world, when Christ's kingdom is finally ushered in – with saving power for the repentant, but with flaming destruction for those who have refused the mercy and patience of God. The destruction in Deuteronomy 7 was terrible enough. But it is there to warn us against something worse – the wrath of the Lamb on the final Judgment Day.

19. 1 Samuel 16:24 – God sending evil?

Can you explain this statement that 'an evil spirit from the Lord tormented Saul'?

We must interpret it in the light of the rest of Scripture. For example, three times we are told that God 'gave over' to impurity and depraved thinking the people who pursued such things – it was his judgment upon them (Romans 1:24,26,28). Revelation 22:11 is similar; as judgment time approaches, 'let the evildoer still do evil, and the filthy still be filthy'. Again we have 1 Kings 22:19–22, where God is spoken of as directing an evil spirit to deceive the prophets of the evil king Ahab.

The point is that God can use an evil instrument to bring about his righteous judgments. Cyrus, the heathen king of Persia, was another such example (Isaiah 44:28). Repeatedly the heathen nations surrounding Israel were used as instruments of divine judgment upon God's own people.

The judgment upon Saul was that his character came to reflect the very evil that he had deliberately pursued. His potential was never realised, and because of his disobedience he became something less, and worse, than a mere neutral nothing.

> Sow an action, reap a habit;
> Sow a habit, reap a character;
> Sow a character, reap a lifetime;
> Sow a lifetime, reap a destiny.

It's terrifying. **Disobedience....hardening....judgment** – that is the pattern. These examples are given to the world for its warning.

20. 1 Samuel 28 – Mediumism supported?

We read that King Saul received a message from God, on visiting the witch at Endor. Could this in some way sanction mediumism on certain occasions?

No, it really can't. The principle with 'difficult verses' of the Bible is that they must be interpreted in the light of the rest of the Bible. Scripture will never contradict Scripture. Even the briefest look at Bible references to necromancy (seeking after the dead) and similar activities, is enough to demonstrate the hostility of God towards mediumistic practices (see chapters 16 and 69).

In this instance, the medium herself declared that such practices had been banned by Saul himself, in his capacity as king (1 Samuel 28:9).

Your question implies that Saul received a message from the Lord through his visit to the medium. No. *Saul had already enquired through the legitimate means available,* and we read, 'The Lord did not answer him, either by dreams, or by Urim or by prophets' (1 Samuel 28:6). This was a mad act of desperation, Saul now turning to hell for an answer.

If you insist on getting an answer from somewhere, the terrifying thing is that you are likely to get it. No resorting to occultism is ever going to prove beneficial, and this occasion was no exception. Samuel – or should we say the spirit masquerading as the departed Samuel – has nothing but doom to impart to Saul. The final commentary on the action taken by Saul is given in 1 Chronicles 10:13,14: 'So Saul died for his unfaithfulness; he was unfaithful to the Lord in that he consulted a medium, seeking guidance, and did not seek guidance from the Lord'. The entire exercise was an entry into the realm of the forbidden.

21. 1 Kings 20:30 – Puzzling numbers?

I cannot understand some of the soaring statistics of the Bible. How could 27,000 people be killed by a falling wall (1 Kings 20:30)?

How indeed? If that figure is correct, then the population of the city of Aphek must have been denser than even that of Hong Kong, with its one person per square yard.

Naturally, Bible critics love these posers, while some earnest believers clutch at the possibility of earthquakes to support these accounts. But surely there is another explanation. After all, what writer with any sense would solemnly report of a bus crash, that all 20,000 passengers were killed?

The scholar John Wenham has pointed out – for those of us who do not read Hebrew – that the word for 'thousand' in early Hebrew (in which there were no vowels) would have been identical to the word for *fully armed soldier*. It is likely then that, somewhere along the line of copyists, the text became confused and 'soldiers' became 'thousands'. In this case the sentence would tell us that twenty-seven soldiers died in this particular incident.

22. Isaiah 9:6 – Jesus the Father?

Doesn't one of Christ's titles 'Everlasting Father' call into question the whole Christian concept of the Trinity?

This is a question that is sometimes asked by adherents of non-Trinitarian religious outlook. No, this text doesn't undermine the truth of the Trinity (see chapter 22). The way to understand this title, 'Everlasting Father', is to look back to Isaiah chapter 8, and to the same messianic figure, albeit with a different name, 'Immanuel' (*God with u*s: vv.8 and 10).

Here, this person – the same as that portrayed in Isaiah 9 – declares, 'Behold, I *and the children whom the Lord has given me* are signs and portents in Israel from the Lord of hosts, who dwells on Mount Zion' (Isaiah 8:18). The 'children' that Christ would have would be of the kind that are 'given' – for him to save, look after and have fellowship with (see also John 17: 6,12).

Indeed Isaiah 8:18 is directly quoted in the New Testament as words of Christ: *'Behold, I and the children God has given me'* (Hebrews 2:13).

Thus we are to understand the term **Father**, in Isaiah 9:6 in the context of its surrounding passage, namely of the wonderful comfort that Jesus Christ was to bring to the people who walked in darkness. As the hymn puts it:

> Father-like, he tends and spares us
> Well our feeble frame he knows
> In his hands he gently bears us,
> Rescues us from all our foes
> Alleluia! Alleluia!
> Widely as his mercy flows.

23. Psalm 58:6 – Break their teeth!

Are we supposed to be in agreement with the Psalmist when he cries out for vengeance on his enemies, as in Psalm 58:6, 'Break the teeth in their mouths'?

We should welcome the alternating moods that we find in the psalms; there is awe, praise, lament, meditation, despair, sorrow – *and rage*. This feature smartly hits on the head the shallow sentiment that all life with God is to be one of non-stop praise.

Definitely not. The Christian life is not lived on a single plateau of outlook and emotions, and the psalms serve as our correction.

True, we would not necessarily sing in church what have come to be known as 'the imprecatory psalms'. It is not that they have no place in inspired Scripture; the reason is that we would not easily trust ourselves to sing them with the proper jealousy for the name and honour of God that ensured their inclusion in God's Book.

For, although the psalmist will come out with such expressions as 'If only you would slay the wicked, O God!' (Psalm 139:19), he is never governed by an animosity to evil people that is purely *personal*. He longs for the destruction of evil – and, if necessary, for that of those who refuse to repent. *God's enemies are his own enemies*.

If we could really see people as God sees them, we could echo even the imprecatory psalms with integrity. It is because I distrust myself, that I am careful about doing it.

24. Matthew and Luke – Jesus' genealogy?

It is difficult to understand the discrepancies between Matthew and Luke, in their listings of Jesus' ancestral line.

Yes, there are noticeable differences. Compare Matthew 1:1–17, with Luke 3:23–38. The first obvious difference is that Matthew works forwards, while Luke works backwards. The second difference is that Matthew doesn't go back further in time than Abraham, while Luke traces Jesus' ancestry right back to Adam.

A third difference is that Matthew seems to concentrate largely on the line that connects with *Joseph*, the legal father of Jesus; Luke appears to work through ancestors of *Mary* – though we note that both Gospel writers make plain that Joseph was not the natural father of Jesus (Matthew 1:16; Luke 3:23).

The whole point of Jesus' genealogy is fourfold: first, Jesus was a real **Man** – a part of the human race – not a Greek-style mythological figure; secondly, he is **Messiah** – hence Matthew's opening reference to the kingly David; thirdly, because Luke's line goes back to Adam, Jesus is **World Saviour** of the entire human race; and fourthly, because Luke's line ends in God himself, Jesus is publicly introduced as **Son of God**.

25. Luke 2:2 – Quirinius who?

Was Luke mistaken in identifying 'Quirinius' as the governor of Syria when Jesus was born? Various sources indicate that he was governor when a census was organised much later, in about 6AD.

Certainly, this is what is widely argued – the 'problem' being that Jesus was born around 6–4 BC. But notice Luke's wording about the census ordered by Caesar Augustus:

> This was the **first** registration when Quirinius was governor of Syria (Luke 2:2).

So there was more than one registration – and this makes sense, since Caesar Augustus reputedly had a passion for organisation and annotation. The second census was indeed in AD6, and Luke makes mention of it in Acts 5:37. He knew! In addition, the scholar William Ramsay draws attention to a certain governor of Syria, who features in a manuscript called *Lapis Tibertinus.*

It is basically an inscription, recording the career of a distinguished Roman officer. Because the document has been mutilated, the officer's name cannot clearly be established – but the fragment contains a statement that when he became imperial Legate of Syria, Quirinius entered upon that office **'for the second time'**. Ramsay tells us that he was appointed a Legate of Syria between 10 and 7BC.

It is not 100 per cent proof – but the fact of *two* registrations, coupled with the knowledge that a prominent Roman became Legate of Syria *twice* – and that furthermore he first took on the job between 10 and 7BC, adds up to compelling evidence that Luke, the meticulous historian, got his facts right.

26. Irreconcilable infancy stories?

It seems impossible to make Matthew's and Luke's stories of Jesus' birth and infancy fit with one another, especially at Luke 2:39.

And yet – as with the accounts of the resurrection (see chapter 50) – patient study reveals an integrated picture. Let's do it step by step.

After the announcement about John the Baptist's birth (Luke 1:5–25) comes that about Jesus – to Mary (Luke 1:26–38), and to Joseph (Matthew 1:18–25). The birth itself is stated factually in Matthew 2:1, and descriptively in Luke 2:1–7. Next, chronologically, are the angels and shepherds (Luke 2:8–20), and eight days later the circumcision and presentation in the Temple at Jerusalem (Luke 2:21–39).

Here comes your problem at verse 39! It reads as though the holy family returned immediately to Nazareth and not to Bethlehem, where – Matthew tells us – there took place the visit of the Magi, followed by the flight to Egypt and eventual return (Matthew 2:1–23). That in itself is no problem; the advantage of having four Gospel writers is precisely because they do fill in gaps for each other. The problem is that *chronologically*, Luke appears to assume an immediate return to Nazareth.

The problem is solved once we realise that at this point Luke is not writing chronologically, but *religiously*. Throughout his Gospel he's concerned to demonstrate that the events of Jesus' life all took place in exact accordance with the requirements of the law of God (for example, Luke 1:6; 2:22–24; 23:56). Here in verse 39, the stress should be on the word *everything*. This would then give the sentence the sense, 'It was **only** after doing everything required by the law that they returned to Nazareth'.

27. Matthew 2:23 – A non-prophecy?

I'm baffled by Matthew's mention of Nazareth, and of the non-existent prophecy, that Jesus would be called a Nazarene.

Let's look at the text: 'And (Joseph) went and lived in a town called Nazareth. So was fulfilled what was said through the prophets: "He will be called a Nazarene"' (Matthew 2:22,23 ESV).

This is the first time that Matthew has mentioned Nazareth. His mention of 'the prophets', rather than 'a prophet', is the first clue. It suggests that Matthew is imparting the overall message of prophets *generally*, as to Jesus' origins as 'a Nazarene'.

And what of Nazareth? The town is nowhere mentioned in the Old Testament; it was a nothing place. *This is a second clue.* The great fifth century scholar Jerome followed his Jewish contemporaries, in connecting Matthew 2:23 with Isaiah 11:1, **'There shall come forth a shoot from the stump of Jesse, and a branch (or off-shoot) from his roots shall bear fruit.'** The word for the lowly 'branch' in that verse is *Netzer.*

But so is the Hebrew form of the name **Nazareth***.* For the record, this was powerfully argued by the German Protestant scholar Hengstenberg (1802–1869), and was accepted as proven by Johann Winer of Leipzig. *Thus, what is a non-descript 'off-shoot' name of a small-time town is identical with the humble 'branch' description of the Messiah in Isaiah 11.* Now it becomes a thrill to read the prophecy! Similar 'branch' language for the Messiah (though using a different Hebrew word) appears in Jeremiah 23:5; 33:15; Zechariah 3:8; 6:12.

Further terms, reflecting the lowly profile of the Messiah, occur in Isaiah 53:2 and Ezekiel 17:22, and are worth studying. Centuries later, Nathaniel was to ask, 'Can anything good come from *Nazareth*?' (John 1:47). So here is the son of an artisan, a 'Nazarene'....an off-shoot figure from unknown *Branch-Town* – that is the image! Yet that, prophetically, was the chosen style of Jesus, the world's Messiah.

28. Matthew 5:21,22 – Talk fit for Hell?

**I don't understand Christ's words, that someone who says
'You fool' will be in danger of the fire of hell. Isn't that
very extreme?**

In this passage, Jesus is outlining three escalating grades of
offence, and the liabilities they incur. He's contrasting the
rigid external observance of God's law with the *spirit* of the
law and its inner meaning. So adultery in the heart is still
adultery (vv.27,28).

The old law, said Jesus, was 'Do not murder' (v.21). Now
he is taking it deeper. What does **God** think about murder –
or, indeed about murder in the making? In point of actual fact,
no one who was 'angry with his brother' was going to be
hauled before the courts, and Christ's listeners would have
known that. And what person calling another, *Raca!* – or 'You
nitwit' – would be brought before the Council in Jerusalem?
And to write someone off (which was what 'Fool' in its
stronger meaning evidently meant) – who cared? True; they're
only illustrations — **but what was going on inside?** It's *that*,
that concerns God.

With the outward/inward principle in mind, we could put
it like this: someone who commits either of the first two
offences is, in God's sight, on the same sort of level as someone
who, in human terms, has to be brought before a local council
or the supreme court. **But if you are sitting in the judgment
seat yourself, and pronouncing someone else a cursed fool,
in the sense of wanting to see them dead and on the rubbish
tip, you are in danger of that judgment backfiring, and so
ending up on the tip yourself.** What Jesus is doing is
establishing a principle. Murder in the heart is murder in the
sight of God. *Hatred of others is never to be the mindset of any
member of the kingdom.*

29. Matthew 5:48 – 'Be perfect'?

I feel very far indeed from being 'perfect', as Jesus commands us to be. It seems impossible. What did he mean?

He meant exactly that. Can you imagine Jesus – the purest of all – saying to his followers, 'Could you please try to sin a little *less*?' However, we do at least aim at perfection *jointly*, within the membership of the church: **'...until we all reach unity in the faith and in the knowledge of the Son of God and become mature, attaining to the whole measure of the fulness of Christ'** (Ephesians 4:13). Are you actively involved in a local church? We cannot grow in maturity and perfection unless we are.

We know that we will not attain 'perfection' in this life. The apostle Paul himself acknowledges this: '...not that I have already obtained all this, or have already been made perfect, but I press on....' (Philippians 3:12).

Think of the old-style Marxists, with their dream of a utopian ideal, attainable in this life. *They were always going to be disillusioned.* We Christians don't think like that at all! We are making perfection our aim, knowing that it is not achievable in this life. Now we can live with that tension, **once we understand it** (see chapters 29 and 93). It's not that we settle for 95 per cent; otherwise, mentally, we are already backsliders! But it is our prayer for each other (Hebrews 13:20,21), as we make likeness to Jesus Christ the aim of our whole lives.

30. Matthew 10:8 – 'Raise the dead'?

I have heard someone speak on the verse, 'Heal the sick; raise the dead, cleanse those who have leprosy, drive out demons'. These, he said, we must do because they are commands of Christ – and he directed us to Matthew 28:19 '....teaching them to obey *everything* I have commanded you.' Was the speaker right?

Well....did the speaker also mention the other commands in the previous two verses of Matthew 10? *'Do not go among the Gentiles or enter any town of the Samaritans.'* If he was going to include those commands among the things that Christ desires us to obey, then his talk would have run into difficulties.

There would have been other commands too, in the same passage, that would have been hard to put into effect: *'Do not take along any gold or silver or copper in your belts; take no bag for the journey....'* etc.

It is as we look at the context of this passage that we can recognise these as specific instructions for the first mission that Christ's twelve chosen apostles were sent out on. They do not necessarily apply to every believer. **If we get the context right, we are likely to get the application right.**

31. Matthew 10:23 – A mistake by Jesus?

How do we explain sentences such as, 'Truly, I say to you, you will not have gone through all the towns of Israel before the Son of Man comes' (Matthew 10:23)?

This is a case of 'prophetic foreshortening' in which the several events associated with Christ's triumphant return (his death, resurrection, ascension and gift of the Spirit) are all lumped together under the over-arching event in which they culminate; namely, his return in glory.

It happens elsewhere in the Bible, for example in **Matthew 24**, where the destruction of Jerusalem (the near event) is somehow telescoped with – and foreshadows – the affairs clearly relating to the end times. It's similar to **Matthew 16:28**: 'There are some standing here who will not taste death before they see the Son of Man coming in his kingdom'. In that instance, Peter, James and John were to be privileged with a 'preview' of the kingdom – of the end times – in the glory of the Transfiguration of Jesus that immediately followed his words, and during which the figures of Moses and Elijah spoke with Christ about his approaching death (Luke 9:30,31).

If we were to paraphrase Matthew 10:23, it could run, *When they persecute you in one town, flee to the next; for I solemnly assure you that the time is short – you won't get through all the towns of Israel before the event of my coming in glory gets initiated. The whole process is just about to start!*

32. Matthew 11:12 – Condoning force?

Please explain: 'From the days of John the Baptist until now the kingdom of heaven has suffered violence, and the violent take it by force'. Is this persecution or what?

It's not persecution. There's a clue in the words, 'From the days of John the Baptist' – because John was a 'forceful' preacher indeed. Perhaps this was partly because he was a transitional figure, bridging the two great eras of the Old and New Testaments. So it was a time of urgency – and opportunity.

John's preaching had led to a great deal of enthusiasm, and people were flocking around Jesus – not so much with a physical violence, *but with the violence of people in earnest.* Take the woman with the haemorrhage (Luke 8:42–48). With the Levitical law against her she would have had to fight her way through the crowd to get to Jesus' side.

There were those who let their paralysed friend down through the roof, to bring him to Jesus (Mark 2:1–12). There was the blind beggar, Bartimaeus, who, by his shouting for help, was able to bring Christ's walk through Jericho to a standstill (Mark 10:46–52).

The difficulties were so many, the possibilities were so great, and the opportunities were so fleeting, that those with everything **against** them, won the kingdom by the violence of their determination. Ironically, those religious leaders with everything going **for** them, lost the kingdom. They hadn't even seen it.

33. Matthew 12:38–41 – The sign of Jonah?

The sign of the prophet Jonah to Jesus' unbelieving hearers poses a problem; the body of Jesus was *not* in the grave for 'three days and three nights'. He would only have spent two nights in the tomb – that is, if he was buried on the Friday.

The sentence in question is 'For as Jonah was three days and three nights in the belly of a huge fish, so the Son of Man will be three days and three nights in the heart of the earth' (Matthew 12:40).

However, by the accepted Jewish way of reckoning, even the smallest portion of the period covering a day and a night counted as the whole period. In this way, a whole day and part of two other days would be counted as three days and three nights.

In the book of Esther, for example, we learn that the young Queen appeals for a fast to be observed on her behalf, during which no one will eat or drink for three days, night or day. Then we read that, **'On the third day Esther put on her royal robes'**, the fast being over (Esther 4:16–5:1). Only two nights had elapsed. But in Jewish thinking three days and three nights would have been crossed off the calendar.

There is no problem, then, with the sign of the prophet Jonah, when – as worshippers say of Christ, in the Creed – 'On the third day, he rose again from the dead'.

34. Matthew 21:7 – A clumsy invention?

At Jesus' entry into Jerusalem, it seems that Matthew mistakenly interpreted the prophecy of Zechariah 9:9 as referring to two animals on which the coming Messiah would sit, and so *invented* both the donkey and her colt, to fit the prophecy (Matthew 21:9).

No, nothing of the sort; Matthew was not the dumb Bible hack that some modern scholars have taken him to be. It is we who are the dim ones!

True, Zechariah 9:9 is a piece of Hebrew parallelism – in that the coming king would be mounted, literally, 'on a donkey, *even on the foal of a beast of burden*'; that indicates **one** animal, not two. But then it is alleged that Matthew misread this to mean two animals, and so clumsily invented a second animal to tie in with the prophecy.

The critics need to read their Bibles more carefully. The far more natural understanding of Matthew 21 is that Matthew – as an alert eyewitness of Christ's entry to Jerusalem – *was already aware of two animals, the colt and its mother.* Certainly, in his Gospel he quotes Zechariah 9:9, which establishes an important link with ancient prophecy. He then relates how the disciples **'brought the donkey and the colt'** (v.7). But is this last sentence a *direct* reference to Zechariah 9:9? No, only an indirect one.

Both 'donkey and colt' in verse 7 are a reference back to the *earlier* part of the passage, where (v.2) the disciples are told by Jesus to go to the village where they would 'find **a donkey tied, and a colt with her**'. 'Untie them and bring them to me,' said Jesus. It would hardly do to separate a colt from its mother, so both are brought. Obviously Jesus would have ridden on the colt, while the mother followed behind. The end of verse 7 – *and he sat on them* – refers to the cloaks, *not* the two animals – as some fatuously have credited Matthew with saying.

All Matthew's critics appear, amazingly, to have overlooked the obvious direct connection made between verses 2 and 7.

35. Matthew 24:36 – The unknown date?

Why didn't Jesus know the date of his return? How does this affect his deity?

The sentence reads, 'But concerning that day and hour, no one knows, not even the angels of heaven, nor the Son, but the Father only' (Matthew 24:36 ESV). A reference like this gives us an ideal occasion to speak about the different *functions* within the Trinity.

It was Christ's responsibility – as the one within the Godhead who was sent into our world – only to say and teach those things that he had been sent to say (John 8:28; 12:49,50). Since the date of the Second Coming was not a part of such teaching, but fell within the category of things that come within the Father's domain, the date is not a part of Jesus' consciousness.

The whole point of a Trinity of Persons in one Being is that, although they are of the same essential nature, they are *not* identical in the **functions** they carry out in the divine mission. It is neither inferiority nor inequality that defines the Persons; the basic difference is in the roles they fulfil.

36. Matthew 27:52 – Tombs opening up?

Please explain why, when Jesus died, the rocks were split, the tombs were opened and some of the departed saints were seen in Jerusalem.

We should not be too surprised at the disturbance of both the physical and spiritual realms by the death of the Son of God; the tearing in two of the temple curtain from top to bottom, the earthquake, the disturbance of the tombs and the appearing of many departed 'holy people' (NIV). All this is related in Matthew 27:50–54.

Were these 'saints' (ESV) followers of Christ; disciples who had already passed to their graves, such as Simeon who had once held the infant Jesus in his arms (Luke 2:25–35)? It seems so. The disturbance, and then the appearances, come as a dramatic portent, indicating that Christ's death (and subsequent resurrection) *affected* the unseen world of the dead as nothing had ever done before.

As James Stalker wrote, 'It was not unnatural....that some of the dead in their excitement and eagerness, should even press back over the boundaries of the other world' (*The Trial and Death of Jesus Christ,* Hodder and Stoughton, 1984, p.275). This was not the final resurrection of the dead, of course. But it was an illustration of the truth that Christ has the keys of death and Hades (Revelation 1:18). As Alfred Edersheim, of Jewish background, once expressed the effect of Christ's death, **'A shudder ran through nature'.**

37. Mark 15:25 – The third or sixth hour?

The Gospel of Mark states that Jesus was crucified at the third hour. Even modern versions do not deviate. Yet from the other Gospels we know that the crucifixion took place at the sixth hour.

First, we must salute the integrity of the scholars, whose work it is to establish exactly what the text of Scripture says: *'And it was the third hour when they crucified him'* That clearly differs from the other Gospel accounts. Various explanations have been offered, but Jerome's of the fifth century seems to be the best.

In the earliest Greek manuscripts the numerals *Third* and *Sixth* would have looked very similar. 'Third' is shown by a simple Gamma letter – like a capital L upside down. 'Sixth' is shown by *exactly the same figure* – but with a tiny crossbar across the vertical stem – like a continental *seven* back to front. It is called the Di-gamma.

Now we can see what probably happened. Somewhere in the long process of copying from manuscript to manuscript, one copyist forgot to put in the tiny crossbar, and the Di-gamma was inadvertently changed into a Gamma.

It hasn't changed any doctrine, and no careful reader is taken in. Indeed Mark himself begins the three hours of darkness (v.33) at the same 'sixth hour' as the other writers. But this does seem to be the explanation.

38. Luke 12:51 – Division through Christ?

Jesus once said that he had come not to bring peace, but division. But isn't Jesus the *'Prince of Peace'*?

Yes, he is (Isaiah 9:6); Christ is the only Person big enough to unite people of every culture under a single banner (see chapter 90).

1. Christ's is a mission of peace and unity. This comes through from the announcing angels' *song* ('...on earth peace...' Luke 2:14); from Zechariah's *prayer* ('to guide our feet into the way of peace' – Luke 1:79), and from Peter's *sermon* ('the Good news of peace through Jesus Christ' – Acts 10:36). Christ has come in peace, not to bludgeon the world into submission, but to win us, through the appealing power of suffering love.

2. Christ's is a mission of truth and judgment. The context of the text in question, Luke 12:51, is one of judgment; Jesus had come to a world of rebels that would reject its only Saviour. *And people are free to choose.* We shouldn't be surprised then at the divisions in every society and family, between those who accept Christ and those who refuse him.

3. Christ's is a mission of hope and patient love. We see this in the amazing diversity of the worldwide church. *How could Jews and Gentiles, for example, ever be united?* Yet Paul could write of them that Christ 'is our peace, who has made the two one, and has destroyed the barrier, the dividing wall of hostility' (Ephesians 2:14).

Jesus is truly the Man of Peace. But his is not a sentimental ideal. Such peace is based on truth; hence the sting in the tail of Luke 12:51.

39. John 1:9 – Is this universalism?

In John 1:9 we read, 'The true light, which enlightens everyone, was coming into the world.' It has been claimed that this means that all are incorporated in God's salvation.

The answer is that, while John 1:9 is an indication of the universal *extent* of Christ's light, the rest of the chapter makes plain that not all are going to accept his light.

The light of Christ is **the light of truth**, original, and unborrowed. Jesus is not simply a 'new' light, or *another* light; he is the true light – as contrasted with the many counterfeit, imperfect and transitory lights. His is also **the light of hope**, for, as 'light of the world', he could promise that *'whoever'* followed him would never walk in darkness (John 8:12).

Christ's light is also **the light of judgment**. When light comes into a room, the dust is shown up; the spiders retreat under the beds. So, when Jesus came, 'people loved the darkness rather than the light (John 2:19 ESV).

So there is no universalism here. Not all will be saved, because not all will respond to the light of Jesus Christ.

40. John 13:1 – When did Jesus die?

There seems to be disagreement between John's Gospel and the other Gospel writers, over when the Passover and Last Supper took place, the day before Jesus died. Why this discrepancy?

Matthew, Mark and Luke are agreed that Jesus met with his disciples for the Passover meal the day before his crucifixion, and that he died on the Jewish fifteenth day of Nisan (Matthew 16:17–30; Mark 14:12–26; Luke 22 7–23).

But John's account reads differently: 'Now **before** the feast of the Passover, when Jesus knew that his hour had come to depart out of this world to the Father, having loved his own who were in the world, he loved them to the end. During supper....' (John 13:1,2).

In John's account, it appears that the Last Supper was held on an earlier day than the Jewish Passover. But another – and completely valid way – of reading the Greek text is to couple the words 'Jesus knew' with 'before the feast of the Passover...' Then the text would read – as it does in the *Twentieth Century New Testament*:

'Before the Passover Festival began, Jesus knew that the time had come for him to leave the world and go to the Father. He had loved those who were his own in the world, and he loved them to the last...'

This reading now makes a very moving 'prologue' to the entire passion narrative that follows. This is how the Sinaitic Syriac text presents the Greek, and many of the early Christian preachers such as Chrysostom and Cyril of Alexandria, understood it in this sense. In which case there is no discrepancy.

41. John 14:12 – Greater works?

Is the age of miracles past, or ought we to be expecting increasing miracles, on the basis of John 14:12?

Here are these well-known words of Jesus: 'Truly, truly, I say to you, whoever believes in me will also do the works that I do; and greater works than these will he do because I am going to the Father.'

This text was once quoted to me in a phone-in radio programme, by a man who interpreted John 14:12 as an encouragement to expect greater physical miracles than Jesus ever performed. But the most dramatic miracle that he could personally vouch for was the dramatic healing of a cut finger.

I told him that I was glad his finger was better, but then I went on to point out that no one, in the whole of history, has ever performed greater physical deeds than Jesus, either in quality or quantity. The healing of a storm with a word, the cleansing of leprosy sufferers at a touch, the raising of a man four days in the grave by a command....there has to be another interpretation of this wonderful saying.

There is. The clue is in the surrounding context – the coming of the Holy Spirit in power, following Christ's 'going to the Father'. With the globalising of the gift of the Spirit and the new birth, Christ's followers on every continent would be accomplishing deeds greater than Christ's – not in terms of physical quality, but rather **deeds of a superior dimension altogether.** As a preacher once put it, *'The 3,000 converted at Pentecost was a greater deed than the feeding of the 5,000.'*

42. John 14:28 – The 'greater' Father?

'The Father is greater than I.' This is often quoted by those who want to disprove the deity of Christ. What is behind these words?

As far as full deity is concerned, the words 'must be interpreted in regard to the absolute relations of the Father and the Son *without violation of the one equal Godhead*' (B.F. Westcott).

Read the words: 'If you loved me, you would have rejoiced, because I am going to the Father; for the Father is greater than I.' Evidently, the disciples ought to have been glad that Jesus was departing – for he was going to the Father's side, where, on their behalf, the full resources of the Godhead would be at work!

This is born out by a preceding verse in the same passage: 'The Helper, the Holy Spirit, whom the Father will send in my name, he will teach you all things...' (v.26). Here we have one of many New Testament texts that combine *all three Persons of the Trinity in a single sentence*. And they are all doing different things. The New Testament teaches that our salvation is **authorised** by the Father, **achieved** by the Son and **activated** by the Holy Spirit.

'My Father is greater than I.' The context shows that Jesus is not speaking *ontologically* here – that is, in terms of the essential being and nature of God – but rather *functionally*; he is speaking of the mission and work of God. So Jesus never sends the Father to do anything (v.24); that is simply not his function within the work of the Godhead. It is the Father who sends the Son – and it is to the Father's side that the Son will return. It is in that functional sense that the Father is 'greater'.

43. Acts 1:18 – Judas' two deaths?

How are we to explain the two very different accounts of Judas Iscariot's death?

Here is Luke's report: 'Now this man bought a field with the reward of his wickedness; and falling headlong he burst open in the middle and all his bowels gushed out...' (Acts 1:18). It has puzzled some that in *Matthew's report* it was the chief priests who bought 'the potter's field' with the thirty pieces of silver that Judas flung at them, and called it 'The Field of Blood' (Matthew 27:3–8).

The explanation is not too difficult. Supposing a sum of money is paid at an auction sale for a Ming porcelain bowl. *Who bought the bowl?* Was it the agent who was present at the auction, or was it the antiques collector who sent him along in his name?

The indication from the Matthew passage is that the legally minded chief priests, having already bought Judas' services of betrayal with the pieces of silver, were reluctant simply to receive them back into the treasury, so used the money to buy a field – *but in Judas' name* – in which to bury Gentiles who had died in the holy city of Jerusalem. Hence the field's change of name.

Some have imagined that Judas, having obtained the field, *then died in it.* But Luke's phrase – 'falling headlong he burst open in the middle' refers not to the middle of the field, but to the middle of Judas' body. What a terrible ending!

44. Acts 20:28 – Did God die?

The phrase in Acts 20:28, that God obtained his church 'with his own blood', has provoked some of my unbelieving friends to ask sarcastically, 'Then did God die?' Where does the answer lie?

It is a remarkable sentence; the only one in the Bible that tells us that God shed 'his own blood'. It is true that *'the blood of his own'* is a possible translation of the Greek text, but it makes little difference. The fact is, the only one true God has suffered personally.

Naturally the words are an irrefutable pointer to the deity of the Lord Jesus Christ – for it was his blood that was shed upon the Cross for the sins of the world.

And when Christ was out there on Skull Hill, it was indeed indivisibly *him*, the God-Man who was dying there. At no point in his ministry or death can we say, 'This is now the human side of him at work; now it is his divine nature that is on display.' Peter could preach of 'Jesus Christ of Nazareth whom you crucified' (Acts 4:10), but Paul can equally write of those who 'crucified the Lord of glory' (1 Corinthians 2:8).

We are given an amazing insight into the relationships within the divine Trinity, as we take in that it was **the eternal Son** who died upon the Cross, enduring the anger of the Father in his own Person – in the place of us who deserved to face the wrath ourselves.

Did God die? Our respectful answer should be, **'You tell me. Who IS this Jesus, who died on the Cross – for you?'**

45. Romans 9:4,5 – Two-track covenant?

When we read of all the riches of the Jewish covenant, why can't we leave the Jews alone – with their own covenant as enough for them?

That is certainly argued by some. But even the description of Romans 9:4,5 is written in anguish by Paul – himself an ethnic Jew – in view of the failure of Israel to obey the covenant. The doors of the covenant, he argues, have now been opened wide to embrace all, both Jews and Gentiles, who obey the international Gospel of God's free grace in Christ.

To advocate a two-covenant theology – one for Jews and the other for Gentiles – is, in the last analysis, *a denial of the Gospel, and an exercise in anti-semitism.* How dare anyone say that Jewish people should be excluded from the all-embracing Gospel! The whole point of Romans 9–11 is to establish 'Israel' as a very precious description of the entire body of believers in Christ, both Jewish and Gentile. The importance of the olive tree image in Romans 11:17–24 **is that it is a single tree** – into which can be *grafted* the 'wild' olive branches of Gentile believers, and into which can be regrafted *back* Jewish believers who accept Christ as the fulfilment of the Covenant.

Christ's purpose was to bring Jew and Gentile together in a single covenant – 'to create in himself one new man out of the two, thus making peace, and in this **one body** to reconcile both of them to God through the cross, by which he put to death their hostility' (Ephesians 2:15,16).

FOR FURTHER STUDY: An exposition of Romans 9, by Paul Blackham: Tape C104/8a from the All Souls Church catalogue: vestry@allsouls.org.

46. Romans 14:10 – Are Christians judged?

How true is it that Christians must face the judgment seat of God? Didn't Jesus teach that believers escape the judgment?

The evidence is massive. 'There is therefore now no condemnation for those who are in Christ Jesus' (Romans 8:1). Like an approaching threatening thundercloud that the winds deflect away, so the judgment of God that had us placed under his wrath has been intercepted by himself, and removed in the dying love of Christ. It is not that we *shall* be saved at the last. We have *already* passed from death to life (John 5:24).

While, for the believer, the sin question will never be raised again, there are enough indications in Scripture that the Christian will face the searchlight of Christ's enquiring gaze at the last day: *How did you spend your days for me? How did you use your opportunities? How did you grow in character and discipleship?* Here in Romans 14:10, the warning is against wrongful judging of others – in the light of the fact that one day the searchlight will be turned upon *us*!

This seems to be especially true for the teachers and pastoral leaders in God's church – to whom 1 Corinthians 3:10–15 is largely (though perhaps not exclusively) addressed. How are they building the work of God? Is the foundation secure? Will it end up like gold, or only as straw? For those who teach others, there are 'rewards', but there is also the possibility of 'loss' – though not of salvation (v.15).

It may be that the greatest 'reward' is that of knowing that we pleased Christ. Perhaps the greatest 'loss' is the knowledge that so much of what was achieved was a waste of time and self-effort.

47. 1 Corinthians 12:13 – Spirit-baptism?

I sometimes hear talk about the Baptism in the Holy Spirit. Is this something that I, as a Christian, need?

Really and truly, it is something that you, as a Christian *already have*. What we do not necessarily have, day by day, is *the filling of the Holy Spirit*, as an ongoing, repeated experience (see chapter 33). But the Baptism in the Spirit is the **inward reality** of which water-baptism is the **outward sign**:

> For we were all baptised by one Spirit into one body – whether Jews or Greeks, slave or free – and we were all given the one Spirit to drink.
>
> (1 Corinthians 12:13 ESV)

Baptism in the Spirit, as the name implies, is the **spiritual initiation** into the *one body* of believers in Christ.

John the Baptist foretold of the ministry of Christ – who would 'baptise you with the Holy Spirit' (Mark 1:8). The disciples had to wait until Pentecost for this to take place. But from Pentecost onwards there is to be no more waiting for the Spirit to come. The reason is that He has been given, with our acceptance of the Gospel (Acts 2:38,39).

As someone is born again into the Christian life (chapter 28), from day one the Holy Spirit takes up residence within. The message of 1 Corinthians 12:13 is that we 'all' – universally – are made **one** with every believer in sight, from every imaginable background. The emphasis is that of **unity**.

48. 1 Peter 3:19 – A second chance?

This verse has been quoted as supporting belief in a 'second chance' after death for the unrepentant. But is this valid?

No, it really is not. First, the whole weight of Scripture is on the necessity to respond to the claims of Christ *now*. 'I tell you, now is the time of God's favour, now is the day of salvation' (2 Corinthians 6:2). The Gospel promises all seem to be for 'today'. The verse you are quoting reads as follows:

> He was put to death in the body but made alive by the Spirit, through whom also he went and preached to the spirits in prison who disobeyed long ago when God waited patiently in the days of Noah.

The meaning of the verse turns upon the words 'preached' and 'spirits'. **Preach** here is not the word used for evangelism; rather it means *to proclaim as a herald*. The word used for **spirits**, when used by itself invariably describes supernatural beings, never people. This is no proof-text for a second chance.

The picture, then, is of Christ's own spirit, following his death, descending into and invading the unseen spiritual world in order that his supremacy over that whole area of existence might be announced. Regarding the 'spirits', we may take them as symbolic forerunners – from the early days of Noah – of the whole rebellious spiritual realm headed by the Devil.

Postscript: In Acts 19:15, an evil spirit cries out, 'Jesus I know!' *Where did he get to know him?* – 1 Peter 3:19 seems to supply the answer.

49. 1 Peter 3:21 – Baptism saves us?

I have had this verse quoted at me by those who say that salvation is incomplete until baptism has taken place. How true is this?

No, it is a sectarian falsehood. Usually those who hold it go further, and insist that any such baptism that takes place must be baptism into their group, if it is to be valid at all! If it was true, then we would have to maintain that there was a 'works', a *doing* element in salvation. But all Scripture is against such a notion.

The sentence runs: '....Baptism which corresponds to this, now saves you, not as a removal of dirt from the body but as an appeal to God for a good conscience, through the resurrection of Jesus Christ....'

In the previous verse, the apostle has taken Noah's ark as an illustration of salvation; now he is saying that baptism is a parallel picture of salvation. But then he is quick to remind his readers that baptism is no mere external ceremony – it is the powerful Gospel visual-aid of salvation; the visible symbol of the inward reality.

And that gives us the clue to your question. If someone sent us a cheque for £100, we would probably reply, 'Thank you so much for the £100.' Yet all we have received is a piece of paper, a pledge. Nevertheless it is £100 we express gratitude for. Or if you became a disciple of Christ after listening to a sermon on John 3:16, it's not impossible that later you were found saying, *'I was saved by that text'*. It is in that sense that the apostle is saying, 'Baptism now saves you'. Its inward reality is the spiritual gift of forgiveness and of the Spirit.

50. 1 John 5:6 – 'By water and blood'?

What is the meaning of the strange statement that Christ 'came by water and blood, not with the water only, but with the water and the blood'. Is this a reference to the sacraments of baptism and the Holy Communion?

No; otherwise the passage in 1 John 5:6 would have read, 'This is he who *comes* by water and blood'. And even then, it would have been doubtful, for logically it should then read, 'by water *and wine.*'

Is this a reference to the blood and water that came from our Lord's side, at his death? Hardly; it is difficult to see how by this way he 'came'.

This text has a backward feel to it. What are these events if not Christ's **baptism** (at the start of his earthly ministry), and his **death** (at its culmination)? John is spelling it out, in hard, physical terms. There were plenty of heretics around who would cheerfully agree that Christ *came,* but that he was not, at every point, fully human. One brand of Gnosticism held that 'Christ' (as distinct from the human 'Jesus') was certainly present at his baptism, but that his divine nature was withdrawn before the cross had taken place.

So John insists that Christ was fully God and fully human at every stage; that '**He** ['Christ'] came, not with the water [the Baptism] **only**, but with the water **and the blood.**' Without such a conviction there is no assurance that we have a Saviour at all, fully God and fully human at every point.

——— Steps to Peace With God ———

1. God's Purpose: Peace and Life

God loves you and wants you to experience peace and life—
abundant and eternal.

The Bible Says . . .

**"We have peace with God through our Lord
Jesus Christ."** *Romans 5:1, NKJV*

**"For God so loved the world that He gave His
only begotten Son, that whoever believes in
Him should not perish but have everlasting
life."** *John 3:16, NKJV*

**"I have come that they may have life, and that
they may have it more abundantly."**
John 10:10, NKJV

Since God planned for
us to have peace and
the abundant life right
now, why are most
people not having this
experience?

2. Our Problem: Separation

God created us in His own image to have an abundant life. He did
not make us as robots to automatically love and obey Him, but gave
us a will and a freedom of choice.

We chose to disobey God and go our own willful way. We still
make this choice today. This results in separation from God.

The Bible Says . . .

**"For all have sinned and fall
short of the glory of God."**
Romans 3:23, NKJV

**"For the wages of sin is death, but
the gift of God is eternal life in
Christ Jesus our Lord."**
Romans 6:23, NKJV

Our choice results
in separation from God.

Our Attempts

Through the ages, individuals have tried in many ways to bridge this gap . . . without success . . .

The Bible Says . . .

"There is a way that seems right to a man, but in the end it leads to death." *Proverbs 14:12, NIV*

"But your iniquities have separated you from your God; and your sins have hidden His face from you, so that He will not hear." *Isaiah 59:2, NKJV*

There is only one remedy for this problem of separation.

3. God's Remedy: The Cross

Jesus Christ is the only answer to this problem. He died on the Cross and rose from the grave, paying the penalty for our sin and bridging the gap between God and people.

The Bible Says . . .

"For there is one God and one mediator between God and men, the man Christ Jesus." *1 Timothy 2:5, NIV*

"For Christ also suffered once for sins, the just for the unjust, that He might bring us to God." *1 Peter 3:18, NKJV*

"But God demonstrates his own love for us in this: While we were still sinners, Christ died for us." *Romans 5:8, NIV*

God has provided the only way . . . we must make the choice . . .

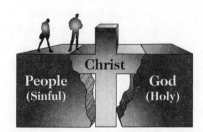

4. Our Response: Receive Christ

We must trust Jesus Christ and receive Him by personal invitation.

The Bible Says . . .

"Behold, I stand at the door and knock. If anyone hears My voice and opens the door, I will come in to him and dine with him, and he with Me." *Revelation 3:20, NKJV*

"But as many as received Him, to them He gave the right to become children of God, to those who believe in His name." *John 1:12, NKJV*

"If you confess with your mouth the Lord Jesus and believe in your heart that God has raised Him from the dead, you will be saved." *Romans 10:9, NKJV*

Are you here . . . or here?

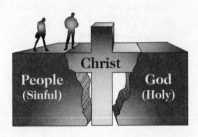

Is there any good reason why you cannot receive Jesus Christ right now?

How to receive Christ:

1. Admit your need (I am a sinner).
2. Be willing to turn from your sins (repent).
3. Believe that Jesus Christ died for you on the Cross and rose from the grave.
4. Through prayer, invite Jesus Christ to come in and control your life through the Holy Spirit. (Receive Him as Lord and Savior.)

What to Pray:

Dear Lord Jesus,
 I know that I am a sinner and need Your forgiveness. I believe that You died for my sins. I want to turn from my sins. I now invite You to come into my heart and life. I want to trust and follow You as Lord and Savior.

     In Jesus' name. Amen.

_____   _____
Date   Signature

God's Assurance: His Word

If you prayed this prayer,

The Bible Says...
"For 'whoever will call on the name of the Lord will be saved.'"
Romans 10:13, NASB

Did you sincerely ask Jesus Christ to come into your life? Where is He right now? What has He given you?

"For it is by grace you have been saved, through faith—and this not from yourselves, it is the gift of God—not by works, so that no one can boast." *Ephesians 2:8,9, NIV*

The Bible Says...

"He who has the Son has life; he who does not have the Son of God does not have life. These things I have written to you who believe in the name of the Son of God, that you may know that you have eternal life, and that you may continue to believe in the name of the Son of God." *1 John 5:12–13, NKJV*

Receiving Christ, we are born into God's family through the supernatural work of the Holy Spirit who indwells every believer. This is called regeneration or the "new birth."

This is just the beginning of a wonderful new life in Christ. To deepen this relationship you should:

1. Read your Bible every day to know Christ better.
2. Talk to God in prayer every day.
3. Tell others about Christ.
4. Worship, fellowship, and serve with other Christians in a church where Christ is preached.
5. As Christ's representative in a needy world, demonstrate your new life by your love and concern for others.

God bless you as you do.

Billy Graham

If you want further help in the decision you have made, write to:
Billy Graham Evangelistic Association,
1 Billy Graham Parkway, Charlotte, North Carolina 28201-0001

A MESSAGE FROM THE BILLY GRAHAM EVANGELISTIC ASSOCIATION

If you are committing your life to Christ, please let us know! We would like to send you Bible study materials and a complimentary six-month subscription to *Decision* magazine to help you grow in your faith.

The Billy Graham Evangelistic Association exists to support the evangelistic ministry and calling of Billy Graham to take the message of Christ to all we can by every effective means available to us.

Our desire is to introduce as many as we can to the person of Jesus Christ, so that they might experience His love and forgiveness.

Your prayers are the most important way to support us in this ministry. We are grateful for the dedicated prayer support we receive. We are also grateful for those who support us with contributions.

Giving can be a rewarding experience for you and for us at the Billy Graham Evangelistic Association. Your gift gives you the satisfaction of supporting an organization that is actively involved in evangelism. Also, it is encouraging to us because part of our ministry is devoted to helping people like you discover and enjoy the stewardship of giving wisely and effectively.

Billy Graham Evangelistic Association
1 Billy Graham Parkway
Charlotte, North Carolina 28201-0001
www.billygraham.org

Toll-free (U.S.): 1-877-247-2426

Billy Graham Evangelistic Association of Canada
20 Hopewell Way NE
Calgary, Alberta T3J 5H5
www.billygraham.ca

Toll-free (Canada): 1-888-393-0003